WARRIOR

THE AMAZING STORY OF A REAL
WAR HORSE

Warrior's White Star

A.J.Munnings

Here is Warrior's head
as drawn by my friend
Munnings.

The likeness is so
striking the expression
so true that I confess
it moves me deeply.
It is "Warrior" that
I see, the real Warrior
with his white star
and his fearless eye.

WARRIOR

THE AMAZING STORY OF A REAL
WAR HORSE

GENERAL JACK SEELY

Illustrated by Sir Alfred Munnings

Introduced by Brough Scott

Foreword by Sir Peter O'Sullevan

RACING POST

DEDICATION
For Jim

Paperback published in Great Britain in 2014 by
Racing Post Books
Axis House, Compton, Newbury, Berkshire, RG20 6NL

Originally published by Hodder and Stoughton in 1934
Reprinted by Racing Post Books in 2011

1 3 5 7 9 10 8 6 4 2

A catalogue record for this book is available from the British Library.

ISBN 978-1-908216-23-6

Jacket design by Jay Vincent
Designed by Fiona Pike

Printed and bound in the Czech Republic by Finidr

www.racingpost.com/shop

CONTENTS

Warrior's mother—How I came to own her—South Africa and Salisbury Plain—The two friends, Cinderella and Maharajah—Maharajah's death—The first foal—Straybit—The birth of Warrior—War—The episode of Isaac—The death of Cinderella.

CHAPTER II

Early days at Yafford—Horse and man—The Jolliffes—On rearing young horses—The first ride on "Sidling Paul."

CHAPTER III

Warrior is introduced to the sea—Racehorse or charger?—In training at Burley-on-the-Hill with Major Hall—His friendship with Freddie Guest.

CHAPTER XII

LIST OF ILLUSTRATIONS

11

FOREWORD

It is a special privilege for this nonagenarian to commend this remarkable story.

Special because my father gave me the book on publication in 1934 when I was already sixteen years into a lifelong attachment to the horse.

The author, General Jack Seely, and Colonel John O'Sullevan had each served throughout the ugly 1914-18 war in France. Likewise the General's amazing Warrior.

"This book," inscribed my father, "is written by a friend of mine and it is a true account from beginning to end."

SIR PETER O'SULLEVAN
BBC racing commentator and journalist

THE PDSA DICKIN MEDAL

Since 1943, the gallantry of animals in war has been honoured through the PDSA Dickin Medal, recognised as the animals' Victoria Cross. Today, it forms part of the world's most prestigious animal awards programme run by PDSA. This helps us fulfil a key element of our founder, Maria Dickin's, vision: to raise the status of animals in society.

Illustrious recipients over the years include pigeons that carried vital messages from behind enemy lines in the Second World War; dogs that located casualties among the rubble during the Blitz and military working dogs that detected bombs and missiles during more recent conflicts.

To mark the centenary of the outbreak of the Second World War, PDSA wanted to ensure that the contributions of all animals that served were duly honoured and recognised. Warrior's incredible story epitomises that contribution and he has been awarded the first Honorary PDSA Dickin Medal.

In backdating this award to Warrior, PDSA wishes to ensure that the gallantry of not only this outstanding horse is recognised, but that it serves as a representation and honour of all the animals that served in the Great War. Warrior displayed gallantry above and beyond the call of duty and was an inspiration to soldiers as they faced their greatest fears against bayonet, bullets, gas and tanks. His truly remarkable story, as documented so wonderfully in this book, is inspiring and heart-warming.

PDSA is UK's leading veterinary charity. With 51 pet hospitals providing vital care for over 470,000 pets each year, there is no other charity comparable to PDSA in terms of the scale and impact we have. PDSA has been a lifeline for millions of sick and injured pets for 97 years – having provided 100 million free treatments to more than 20 million pets in that time.

JAN McLOUGHLIN
PDSA Director General

13

MUNNINGS'S GLORIFICATION OF FLOWERDEW'S CHARGE
30 MARCH 1918.

14

INTRODUCTION

Warrior was a bay Thoroughbred gelding that my grandfather Jack Seely bred from his own mare Cinderella and who was foaled in the spring of 1908 a few miles from our then family home at Brooke in the west of the Isle of Wight. In many ways the real life Warrior is socially the complete opposite of Michael Morpurgo's fictional Joey, the star of *War Horse* who has so beguiled first readers, then theatregoers and now is set to go global in Steven Spielberg's film. And yet …

Joey is the farmboy's friend who is bought at market, conscripted into the Army, is lost and battered through terrible ordeals on the Western Front before a triumphantly happy ending. Warrior is the charger the General bred and rode himself for over 30 years including through all the major battlefields of the Western Front. He was an equine hero who had grooms and batmen to look after him and whose other riders, then and later, included judges, Field Marshals, jockeys and even my mother when her arms were feeling strong. Very different worlds. And yet …

And yet their single most attractive quality is one that is equally shared. It is the simple, unspoken, uncomplaining nobility of the horse from which men and women have drawn such inspiration down the ages. Warrior may have been at the head of the column, not in the ranks, but that only made him more of a target. He may sometimes have had a roof over his head rather than the open sky, but it remains a miracle how he survived all four years of the war from Ypres, to the Somme, Passchendaele, and Cambrai before finally himself leading a cavalry charge which crucially checked the great German offensive in the spring of 1918. The date was 30 March – four years to the day before he went on to win the Lightweight race at the Isle of Wight point-to-point. Not for nothing did the Canadian cavalrymen dub him "The horse the Germans couldn't kill."

His story is one of its time and is quite inconceivable now. It is also written in the argot of the period by a man who epitomises all the old Imperial "King and Country" certainties which seem so outdated now. But at the core of the tale is a belief and a truth that has been worth proclaiming since we humans first tried to form a partnership with our four-legged friends. It is that some of the greatest experiences in history have been achieved from the back of a horse. So before meeting this one, I had better introduce you to the man himself.

By the time my grandfather Jack Seely came to write *My Horse Warrior* (the original title of the book) in 1934 he had already lived about five lives and had exhibited many magnificent qualities even if modesty was not always amongst them. However, those of us who have laughed at the story of him supposedly recommending Warrior for the VC under the simple citation, "He went everywhere I went", know that it would not have been wholly undeserved – for either of them.

Jack Seely, born at Brookehill Hall near Nottingham on 31 May 1868, was indeed a very brave man. Despite the classic Harrow to Cambridge to The Bar gentleman's progress, the proudest achievement of his early life was to row in the lifeboat at Brooke next to his family's home on the Isle of Wight and on 19 October 1881 he won the French "Medaille d'Honneur" for swimming out with a lifeline to the wrecked *Henri et Leontine*.

It was a life of privilege, of service – he was to become an MP and sit in the Cabinet alongside his great friend Winston Churchill – and of horses. As part of his recovery from the injuries sustained

LIFE AT THE FRONT—HORSES DID MUCH OF THE DIRTY WORK.

17

in the *Henri et Leontine* drama, Seely sailed to Wellington, New Zealand, in 1892 and hired horses to trek up through North Island, where rivers still had to be swum and Maori rulers placated. As part of his service with the Hampshire Yeomanry he took his little white Arab Maharajah to Southampton docks in 1900 and embarked with 500 men for the Boer War, albeit having had to dye the horse brown after being first refused for "reasons of camouflage".

How Jack Seely did it all, how he and Maharajah slept side by side in the open Veldt, how he was elected MP whilst still in South Africa, how he made common cause with Winston Churchill, how political drama was followed by military peril and final return have all been related by him in a series of not exactly understated volumes of autobiography bearing such titles as *Adventure* and *Fear and Be Slain*.

For long the received wisdom was to scoff at such apparently blimpish vision, but in recent times there has been a more forgiving mood, and ten years ago I went to explore the glory and the sadness of this particular son of "Imperial Certainty" in my book *Galloper Jack*. Writing it was both a sobering and uplifting experience, revisiting some terrible dramas but being re-challenged by what the spirit of man can do.

And what a horse can do too. Warrior has long been a legend in our family and his ghost trotted with me from page to page. So much so that as public interest latched on to the wonders of Michael Morpurgo's *War Horse* story, I prepared to revisit Warrior and tell the tale myself.

But what a presumption when it has been already told by the man who shared Warrior's life from cradle to his 33-year-old grave. A man who was able to call on his friend Alfred Munnings, the

GUARDS' REVIEW IN HYDE PARK, LONDON, 28 APRIL 1913. WINSTON CHURCHILL, FIRST LORD OF THE ADMIRALTY, WITH JACK SEELY, SECRETARY OF STATE FOR WAR.

WHAT WARRIOR ESCAPED. MUNNINGS'S VERY SOBER STUDY FOR
A MURAL—VERY DIFFERENT FROM THE 'GLORY' PICTURE.

renowned war artist and horse painter, to create unique illustrations
to illuminate the text and which thanks to the Munnings Trust
are reproduced again. A story that has lit up the life of Sir Peter
O'Sullevan, the legendary BBC horseracing commentator, who in
his 94th year immediately penned so elegant a foreword.

So take the time to travel back to Jack Seely and Warrior's side
in 1934. Read this with the odd allowance for hyperbole and for
a wish that horses might always continue to rule the earth. And
at the end I think you will echo the sentiments best expressed by
Ginger McCain as he rushed out to greet Red Rum returning at

QUEEN MARY WITH WARRIOR AND JACK SEELY AT MOTTISTONE DURING COWES WEEK, 1934.

21

Aintree after his record third Grand National victory. Ginger had tears in his eyes at the thought of all the years and the dramas and the glory that he and "Red" had been through. He seized me by the shoulder and said simply: "What a horse!"

BROUGH SCOTT
Sports writer and broadcaster
Surrey, 2011

Celebrating Centenary

Lord Mottistone, who, as General "Jack," commanded the Canadian Corps Cavalry during the war, is shown celebrating a private centenary, at his home on the Isle of Wight, by going for a gallop on his well-known horse, Warrior, to celebrate the fact that their combined ages total 100 years. Lord Mottistone was 70 on May 31. A little subtraction reveals the age of Warrior, to whose exploits his owner has devoted a whole book. (AP.)

100 YEARS BETWEEN THEM.
WARRIOR (30) AND JACK
SEELY (70) TROT OUT AT
MOTTISTONE IN
MAY 1938.

WARRIOR TIMELINE

1908 Spring: Warrior born at Yafford, Isle of Wight
1910 Warrior bucks Jack Seely off on their first ride but they later walk
into the sea
1914 11 August: Warrior lands at Le Havre to join the Allies
on the Western Front
1915 February: Warrior returns to the UK to join the Canadian Cavalry
on Salisbury plain*
1915 5 May: Warrior first off boat in Boulogne
1915 Warrior with the Canadian Cavalry in the trenches near Ypres
1916 1 July: Warrior waiting to "gallop through the G in Gap" in the Battle
of the Somme
1917 March: Warrior in cavalry attack at Guyencourt
1917 September: Warrior stuck in mud at Paschendaele
1917 20 November: Warrior in front line of big Cambrai attack
1918 February: Alfred Munnings arrives to paint the already legendary Warrior
1918 21 March: Last great German offensive. The Canadian Cavalry start
circular retreat
1918 30 March: Warrior leads vital charge at Moreuil Wood, near Amiens
1918 1 April: Seely gassed – Warrior stays as General Patterson's charger
1918 December: Warrior back to Brooke for Christmas
1919 19 July: Victory Parade in Hyde Park
1922 30 March: Warrior wins IOW point-to-point four years to the day
since he led the Moreuil charge
1934 War Veterans Show at Olympia
1934 Munnings at Mottistone
1934 *My Horse Warrior* published by Hodder & Stoughton
1938 Warrior and Seely ride – 100 years combined ages
1941 Warrior dies at Mottistone
2011 *Warrior: The Amazing Story Of A Real War Horse* published
by Racing Post Books
2014 9 July: Philip Blacker bronze statue of Warrior
and Jack Seely unveiled at Carisbrooke Castle
2014 2 September: Warrior awarded PDSA Dickin Medal
at Imperial War Museum

* Right: Winnipeg, the bear cub who came over with the Canadian
Cavalry, went on to London Zoo where he became the inspiration
for AA Milne's 'Winnie The Pooh'.

1934

CHAPTER I

CINDERELLA

Warrior's mother—How I came to own her—South Africa and Salisbury Plain—The two friends, Cinderella and Maharajah—Maharajah's death—The first foal—Straybit—The birth of Warrior—War—The episode of Isaac—The death of Cinderella.

WARRIOR was born within sound of the sea at Yafford, in the Isle of Wight, just twenty-six years ago to-day. His lovely black thoroughbred mother, Cinderella, had been taken along the coast road from my home at Brooke about three weeks before his birth. I well remember "Young Jim" turning up at 9 o'clock one morning, on a long-legged three-year-old, and announcing that he was going to lead her over to that famous little establishment at Yafford where so many good horses have been bred.

I will describe "Young Jim" and his family presently, but first I must tell how Warrior's mother, Cinderella, came to belong to me, and I to her, for, as will be seen in a moment, we were linked together in a great and real friendship.

I had just returned from the South African War, where all of us young men thought we had become preternaturally observant. Each one of us who had commanded advance guards of mounted men during that long struggle, in which we learned to admire

25

our enemies more and more, thought himself the embodiment of Sherlock Holmes. No doubt it was true that anyone who had the lives of a squadron of men and horses committed to his care, leading them forward in that mysterious country—the High Veldt of South Africa—did, indeed, have his wits sharpened to an extraordinary degree. It was a game of everlasting hide and seek. Ultimately the overwhelming superiority was with the English, but locally it was often on the side of the Dutch. All the time an immense advantage lay with the Dutchman, not so much in his knowledge of the country, as in his knowledge of the horse—how to manage him, how to care for him, how to keep him quiet at the tense moment before fire opens, how to prevent him from trembling, or, worst of all, from stampeding when fire opens unexpectedly. All these things the Dutchman knew far better than we did. It was from the Dutch, and especially from the greatest of them all, in the end England's good and faithful friend, General Botha, that I learnt the supreme value of understanding and caring for the horse, and of treating him not as a slave but as a brother.

Whilst writing this little book about Warrior I recall the moment in my life when an Arab of the desert first opened my eyes to the possibilities of companionship with the horse. That was ten years before the time of which I speak; it was in South Africa that I learnt that the Arab's dictum was true.

And so it came about that Cinderella, Warrior's mother, came into my keeping in the strange way that she did, through the power of observation that I had picked up in South Africa.

In August 1902 the yeomanry regiment to which I belonged, the Hampshire Carabineers, was in camp on Salisbury Plain. I had been promoted to command a squadron on my return from the War, and was sitting on the top of Silk Hill, having been ordered to plan a field-day for the following morning.

I was surveying the well-known landscape with my 24-diameter telescope, the present of a famous deer-stalker, which was of constant value to me in South Africa and in the late War, and has been ever since. On my left, as I sat there with my Arab pony, Maharajah, a little cloud of dust caught my eye. The telescope showed me that it was a man galloping at great speed. As he drew nearer I saw that it was an officer in khaki uniform mounted on a black horse with long mane and tail. They passed within three hundred yards of me at the foot of the hill, and I recognised the smooth effortless gallop of a perfectly trained thoroughbred on terms with his rider.

My father had told me that he would give me a charger. My mind was made up. This must be my charger! Clearly the man would not be galloping like this, all alone, unless he knew that his horse was perfectly sound in wind and limb, nor would he be sitting so easily in the saddle unless he were sure that his horse would not attempt to run away with him.

So I jumped on to Maharajah's back and galloped sideways down the hill to try to catch him up. Eventually the black thoroughbred, as I made it out to be, slowed down, and I ranged up alongside the rider.

This was our conversation:

"Would you sell that horse of yours?"

"It isn't a horse, it's a mare."

"I'm sorry, but will you sell that mare?"

"Well, I might."

"How much?"

"Seventy pounds."

"I would have given you ninety or a hundred; but will you ride over to my camp at once?"

"You're an odd young man."

"I'm sorry, but you have a lovely mare."

"Yes, she is a lovely mare. The kindest thing I have ever known."

So we rode back over the hill where I had been sitting, and down to the camp. On the way he told me something of Cinderella's story—how she was a clean-bred mare from County Leitrim, how he had bought her for £60, six months before, from the famous Mr. Field, of Chichester, how she was almost human, and would follow him about like a dog. As he talked Cinderella would cock one ear back, and listen to his voice.

I remembered what my Arab friend had told me, and by that time would have sold all my few possessions in order that Cinderella might be mine.

And so we rode down to our camp on that glorious August morning, and jumped off at my tent.

My faithful orderly of South African days, Smith, came forward and took both horses, and I invited my guest inside to have a whisky and soda. While we sat there waiting for it to come, I asked him again:

"Did you say seventy pounds?"

"Yes, I said seventy."

I wrote him a cheque for eighty and handed it to him.

"But why the extra tenner?"

"Because I am going to keep your lovely Cinderella here, and you can ride back on some other horse which I will lend you."

He laughed at my enthusiasm, and accepted the cheque, protesting as he rode away on the pony I lent him that he would send me back ten pounds any time that I wished.

So Warrior's mother came to belong to me, and, in a curious way, so far as there can be true affinity between man and horse, I to her.

Her story is romantic, and ends on a sad note, but on this first day, without doubt, it can be said that it was a happy chance that brought us two together.

How well I remember on that summer's morning, in camp on Salisbury Plain, leading my new charger to the horse-lines, where about four hundred other horses were tethered by a headstall and a hind leg to long ropes pegged down to the ground. I saw Cinderella looking at me all the time and wondering what was in store for her. By great good fortune, tethered on the very end of the rope was my white Arab pony, Maharajah, that I had ridden constantly for a year and a half in the South African War. He had left the Isle of Wight with me at the end of 1899, and after much trekking over the South African veldt, and many battles, which we now regard as small, but some of which we then regarded as very important, he had returned with me once more in 1901.

I had followed the advice of the Arab chieftain, whose words I quoted at the beginning of this book, in every particular with Maharajah, who was indeed my friend, and would never leave me even when loose and free from all control. He was just such a companion as a dog can be, but more intimate, and a closer friend.

Maharajah whinnied when I came up to the horse lines, then looked round, and saw the beautiful, coal-black mare with the glossy coat and clear, wide-open eye of the Arab. I wondered what would happen, and expected the worst, for Maharajah, like all horses who become friendly with men or women, was jealous of any rival. My faithful groom and orderly, who had been with me and Maharajah during our long service together in South Africa, accompanied me on this adventure. We both made endearing remarks to Maharajah, but I could plainly see a wicked look in his eye. I handed my sleek new thoroughbred to Smith, and told him to tie her up to the head-rope four feet from Maharajah while I went forward, patted his neck, and tried to explain to him that he had a nice new friend coming to see him. He trembled a little, and refused a lump of sugar which I had brought to offer him in order to effect a friendship. Then I stepped back while the tying up of the head-stall and the hind leg was accomplished.

Cinderella never turned her head to look at Maharajah, nor did Maharajah, four feet away, pay the least attention to her. Then I made a mistake. I went forward and fondled Cinderella's head and ears, and with a pat for Maharajah turned about and walked away. I had not gone ten yards when there was a scream; Maharajah had broken his headstall, and had caught Cinderella's wither firmly in his teeth! I dashed back to them, and they were soon separated. It was the first and last occasion on which they quarrelled, for, from that moment, they became inseparable friends. When I rode one the other followed; I have never known two horses so deeply attached to one another.

Human beings will not realise that the affections of horses are much more closely akin to their own than is the case with any other creature. The Arab knows this, and treats them as human beings. Europeans think that the Arabs are, as they phrase it, "mad about horses." It is we and not the Arabs who are mad in our dealings with these the most mysterious, and most lovable, of all God's creatures.

From that moment Cinderella was my constant companion and friend until the outbreak of the recent War. Maharajah showed discernment in his affection for her, for she was the gentlest, kindliest creature that I have ever known, especially beloved by children. She would let my children climb up over her head, and slide down her tail and, still more remarkable, swarm up her tail and slide down over her head. But she had a fine turn of speed, and though only standing fifteen hands, could, I think, have won a good race. At any rate I was often begged to allow her to try.

But this is a book about Warrior, Cinderella's son, and so I must not tell the whole story of his mother, tempted as I am to do so. Briefly her tale is this:

She came back with Maharajah and me to the Isle of Wight, where she was to spend most of her life. Whether it was the change from being one of a "string," that hateful phrase, to being one of two in constant touch with her friend called the "owner," I do not know, but the fact is that this lovely, docile, black thoroughbred became so devoted to me that she could not bear to leave me. My elder children will testify that whenever she saw me she would jump out of any enclosure, even over an iron railing, in order to join me.

As Maharajah became too old to attend manœuvres and staff rides, Cinderella took his place. When I became a Minister, Cinderella came to London with me, and I used to ride her every morning to the Colonial Office, after a gallop round the Park if I got up early enough—a rare occasion. But she did not like London, and was never really happy there. Of course when the Parliamentary recess came we enjoyed ourselves thoroughly in the Isle of Wight, riding over the downs or galloping over the sands at Brooke and Compton, and sometimes taking a day with the Isle of Wight Hunt. But although she could gallop fast, and jump well, I knew she did not care for these days with hounds. What she really loved was to be alone with me in the sun or the rain, and, above all, in the great south-west winds. It was in days of storm that she sprang to life; she loved the strong west wind. I see her now with distended nostrils, black mane and tail streaming, galloping through the gale and rejoicing in her strength.

Meantime her comrade, Maharajah, the white Arab, whom she had first met on Salisbury Plain, and who had been her constant companion in the Isle of Wight, while they were turned out together on the cliff as often as might be, slipped up one frosty morning, crossed his legs and broke his neck. The school-children were all looking on, and Maharajah loved to give them a show, jumping over imaginary obstacles, galloping on his forelegs while whisking his hindquarters round and round as only Arabs can do. It was in doing this particular trick that he slipped on the icy ground and met his end. But Cinderella was looking on too; she was broken-hearted, and wandered listless and gloomy for day after day, re-fusing to take any food offered to her.

Then "Young Jim," my constant adviser in any-thing connected with horses, had a great idea. Obviously so wonderful a creature should have a child, and so in 1906 she was mated with a horse named Likely Bird. She went to Yafford for the event, and, in due course, a handsome son was born within sound of the sea. "Young Jim," and all con-cerned, thought this was the best foal ever seen, but, unfortunately, the brilliant young thing caught a chill of some kind, and died suddenly, to the disappointment of the Jolliffe family, and to the real grief of his mother, Cinderella.

I saw her often at this time, and, though it is difficult for human and equine creatures to communicate with each other, I like to think that she was somewhat consoled by our interviews in those grass fields stretching down to the sea at Yafford. But more real consolation was provided by another mate. This time it was Straybit who was destined to be the father of her foal.

Straybit was an exceptionally bright chestnut. I never saw a better-looking horse. By breeding he had every advantage. His father was Burnaby, his mother was Myrthe.

Before me as I write I see among his ancestors the names of such famous horses as Voltigeur, winner of the Derby and the St. Leger in 1850, Lowlander, The Baron, Stockwell and Pocahontas. Straybit was indeed bred for speed, but it is interesting to note that more than one of those who keep careful account of our great English thoroughbreds have told me that his ancestors include an exceptional number of horses and mares well known for their gentleness and docility.

For although so handsome and so swift, Straybit was of an exceptionally kindly nature. "Young Jim," who looked after him, as well as Cinderella and their child, Warrior, tells me that not only did he ride him in several races, but he was so quiet that he even went to the length of putting him in harness just for fun.

This particular adventure was not a success. Straybit went along quietly enough with this strange

34

thing—a dog-cart—behind him until something displeased him, probably the crupper. In spite of the efforts of "Young Jim" and two other people, Straybit just set to work to get rid of that dog-cart as fast as he could, a feat which he accomplished with no damage to himself, and very little to the men who tried to restrain him, though they found themselves in a ditch; but the dog-cart was never the same again! However, this was the only occasion when Straybit lost his temper.

One very interesting episode in his life occurred in the spring of 1909. He won the Lightweight Race at the Isle of Wight Point-to-Point, the same race that his little son Warrior was destined to win, after four years of the Great War, in 1922. On both occasions "Young Jim" was the successful rider. It will be seen as this story goes on that Warrior's life has been a series of interesting coincidences. I believe the race was run on the same day in both years. Certainly on the second occasion, when Warrior won, the date was the 30th March, which was the anniversary of his greatest ordeal, and most miraculous escape in the Battle of Amiens, in 1918.

But to return to Straybit. In the December after he won the Isle of Wight Point-to-Point he went to the blood-stock sales at Newmarket, where he was bought at a good price by the Austrian Government. I have heard that he was a very successful sire, and sometimes I wonder whether Warrior may not, in the course of the War, have met, at fairly close quarters, his half-brothers and half-sisters, or even his father himself.

35

We do know that the Austrians provided a great number of horses to the German army, so such a happening is not impossible.

However, the main importance of Straybit to Cinderella and to me lay in the fact that he was the father of Warrior.

How well I remember receiving the telegram at the Colonial Office, where I was then installed as Under-Secretary of State, announcing:

"Fine child for Cinderella born at Yafford this morning. Both doing well.—JIM."

My private secretary brought me the telegram, and looked at me narrowly. He was an austere man, R. V. Vernon, a most distinguished civil servant, and until lately our financial advisor in Iraq. I shouted with joy, and then turned on him and told him that Cinderella was a mare. But as he retired demurely I knew that he did not believe a word of what I said!

Yafford is one of the most delightful places that one could choose to possess as a birthplace. The thatched farm buildings where Warrior was born look just the same to-day as they did twenty-six years ago, even to the chickens scratching in the yard outside. Here is an impression of it by my friend, and Warrior's friend, A. J. Munnings, who has caught the atmosphere of it better than I can possibly express it in words.

In due course Warrior was weaned, and with his mother roamed the fields at Brooke and Mottistone, till she once more resumed her duties as my charger.

warrior birthplace
Yafford
A. J. M.

YAFFORD IS ONE OF THE MOST
DELIGHTFUL PLACES THAT ONE
COULD CHOOSE TO POSSESS AS A
BIRTHPLACE. MUNNINGS HAS
CAUGHT THE ATMOSPHERE OF IT
BETTER THAN I CAN POSSIBLY
DESCRIBE IT IN WORDS.

Then, in August 1914, Warrior went to the War with me and Cinderella was left behind in the Isle of Wight, turned out in the big grass fields adjoining Brooke and Mottistone, wherever the pasture was best. Again, as when Maharajah was killed, she became listless and moody, missing not only me, her friend for twelve long years, but her son with whom she had been, with some intervals, for more than four years past. My children did their best to look after her, and to cheer her up, but for the first month or two she seemed inconsolable. However, the World War had a curious consequence for Cinderella and provided her with some consolations.

Warrior and I having gone to the Front, Cinderella spent most of her time alone, turned out in the great field called "Sidling Paul." Now my father had a good breed of very powerful cart-horses, in which he took a great interest. One thing that made it necessary for these cart-horses to be very strong was the existence of the Brooke lifeboat. It took ten horses to haul the heavy boat on its carriage along the loose sand to the point of launching, but even with ten horses, unless each one was powerful, and they all pulled as a team, the boat was liable to get stuck. Such a team was always forthcoming in my father's time, and, indeed, until a year ago, when we replaced the horses with a tractor.

I suppose things were a little disorganised in September 1914, but, whatever the explanation, a very fine entire cart foal was turned out on "Sidling Paul" too. No doubt it was assumed that Cinderella was much too old to have another child, but it happened otherwise.

When I came home on short leave in the summer of 1915 almost the first question I asked was, "How is Cinderella?" The children replied with glee:

"Cinderella has had a baby and we have christened it Isaac."

"Why Isaac?"

"Well, we thought she must be almost as old as Sarah was in the Bible! Come and see him."

So we walked up to the paddock between the house and the church. There was Cinderella, who, seeing me, neighed and cantered up. Sure enough she was followed by a young foal. It had a sweet little head, as all foals have, but the most comically hairy legs and heels! I fondled Cinderella as she rubbed her head against my shoulder, while the foal surveyed us both with interest. I could not help laughing when I looked at its hairy legs, and I am sure Cinderella was hurt, for she turned away from me, and licked her child's shoulder. However, I called him endearing names, and made him suck a lump of sugar, so that Cinderella resumed her equanimity, and walked back with me towards the house.

I went through the kissing-gate into the garden and was walking up the path towards the house when I heard a rat-tat behind me. I looked round and saw that the foal had jumped the iron railing, and was trotting up to us, to the consternation of his mother, who realised that she could not follow.

However, we soon lifted the kissing-gate off its hinges, and restored them to each other.

I had to return to France two days later, and so saw no more of Isaac; and, to my infinite regret, I saw but little more of Cinderella either, for the end of her story is sad. She was devoted to her quaint child; the very fact that everyone laughed about the episode made her more than ever determined to be kind to the little animal. My children and the farm bailiff concur in saying that they never saw a mare so devoted to her foal. But shortly after Isaac had been weaned, his passion for jumping was his undoing. In trying to jump a very high fence out of the paddock he caught his forefeet, fell, and broke his neck.

So Cinderella was more than ever lonely, except for the constant attention of the children.

I did not see her again until 1916. It was late on a summer's evening, and pale shafts of sunlight shone through the trees. As soon as I reached home I asked the children how was Cinderella? They said she seemed rather feeble, and was in the field by the church path. So I walked up there, and saw her, standing very erect with arched neck—I suppose she had heard my step on the gravel path. I gave her a shout, our agreed shout, and she looked my way. I gave another shout, and then she knew. But this time she could not canter; she trotted up to me and gave me a greeting so affectionate, so moving in its intensity that I can never forget it. I talked to her for a long time, stroking her nose, before turning home.

Early the next morning my son Patrick, then a

little boy of eleven, came knocking at my door and shouting:

"Daddy, there is something wrong with Cinderella."

I jumped up, and ran out to the field where I had left her the evening before. There, lying on the church path, was Cinderella. I knew at once that she was dead. I suppose that for all that long year she had waited to see me.

It was a Sunday morning, and we had to pass her body on our way to church. Soon after midday I received the inevitable telegram, which all who served in the War will still remember so well, ordering me to return at once. I left immediately and got back to France the same night. On the Monday Cinderella was buried.

CHAPTER II

WARRIOR

Early days at Yafford—Horse and man—The Jolliffes—On rearing young horses—The first ride on "Sidling Paul."

BUT to return to Cinderella's son, and his early days with his mother.

She was devoted to him. There was nothing very unusual in that, for the mare is devoted to the foal in a higher degree than the mother is to the son in any other species. But the converse is not always true. Nevertheless, Warrior, so the Jolliffes tell me, and I can confirm it from my own observations, was devoted to his mother in a way extraordinary to all who saw them together. This young horse, who was destined to go through ordeals more intense than almost any other horse born at the time, and, by a series of almost miraculous happenings, to escape unscathed, was quite remarkable in the first few months of his life for the affection he showed for his mother.

It was lucky for me that his mother in her turn was so fond of me, and that her son accepted me as a comrade rather than as a master. I say it was lucky, because at the crisis of my life it was my horse Warrior who carried me through from impending disaster to success.

In the first words of this book I have told of my

MUNNINGS NEVER SAW CINDERELLA,
BUT HE HAS DRAWN AN IMAGINARY
PORTRAIT OF HER WITH WARRIOR
WHEN A FOAL WHICH MIGHT HAVE
BEEN MADE ON THE SPOT.

43

conviction that man and horse are an inseparable unit. The ancient sagas of Northern Europe are but a continuance of the beliefs of the Babylonians, the Greeks and the Persians indicating the strange connection between the human and equine races. In our own times I know no one with a greater insight into the nature of this connection than E. R. Calthrop, who had behind him the accumulated experience of hundreds of years of himself and his forebears in the breeding and care of horses. In his book, which he calls *The Horse as Comrade and Friend*, he has discerned the true nature of the strange and romantic relationship between horse and man.

The story of my horse Warrior will show that not only did his vivid personality help me to gain the confidence of thousands of brave men, when without him I could never have achieved it, but that by his supreme courage at a critical moment, he led me forward to victory in perhaps the greatest crisis of the War. That is a high claim to make for any creature. In the course of this book I hope to make it good.

What was the early life of this little fellow? He was independent, aloof from most human beings, unusually devoted to his mother, and ready to attack with embarrassing violence any stranger who sought to approach her. This is what "Young Jim" tells me, "Young Jim" who watched over him during the first few months of his life. As he has already come into the story more than once it may be convenient to explain here who "Young Jim" is.

The Jolliffe family have been established in the Isle of Wight for many generations. When Warrior was born, there were three brothers, all with that mysterious affinity with the horse which, for some strange reason, always runs in families.

First there was "Old Jim," Mr. James Jolliffe, of Shorwell, who for many years hunted the Isle of Wight fox-hounds with great success. At the age of 86 he was still following hounds, and he only died this summer at the age of 89.

Then there was his brother, Doctor Jolliffe, who combined a large practice in the remote south-west part of the island with a practical knowledge of horses and their breeding. When the Government of the day, some thirty years ago, appointed a commission to inquire into the desirability of establishing a Government horse-breeding establishment, they sought the advice of Doctor Jolliffe. One of the members of the commission, the late Lord Harrington, told me that he learned more about the breeding and early care of horses from Doctor Jolliffe, and his brothers Harry and Jim, than from anyone else whom he consulted. Doctor Jolliffe told him that the important thing was that horses should be bred on the appropriate soil with the limestone not too far off—on that even the scientific people agree—but, above all, in a place where there are steep hills and low-lying meadows exposed to the full force of the great south-westerly winds blowing straight off the sea. Lord Harrington was so much impressed with what Dr. Jolliffe had told him that he urged the Government to set up their horse-breeding establishment on the south-west coast of the Isle of Wight. No doubt Dr. Jolliffe was right. Ireland, which produces the greatest horses of all, gives proof enough that the great south-west wind, for some reason we cannot understand, is the thing that makes the young horse live and thrive.

The third Jolliffe brother, Harry, had charge of the small but important stud farm at Yafford.

Of the next generation there was "Young Jim," son of James Jolliffe, who combined the knowledge and love of horses and their psychology possessed by his uncle the doctor, with the love of hounds, and the capacity for getting on terms with his horse possessed by his father. There seems to be no better way of summing up his qualities as a horseman than to say that "Young Jim" has better "hands" than any other man I have ever met.

I have seen him ride yearlings, two-year-olds, three-year-olds, and horses of all successive ages, in the hunting field and in steeplechases. I have never seen him strike a horse in anger, and have never failed to see him get on terms with his horse. It was Warrior's infinite good fortune that he found in "Young Jim" his first friend.

At the Yafford stud farm, only three miles from Mottistone, which the Jolliffes managed, were kept a number of good stallions, by arrangement with the Government. Straybit, Warrior's father, was one of these, and in these ideal surroundings for the upbringing of horses, Warrior spent his early life.

He was a strange little fellow. His mother, as I have

said earlier in this chapter, was more devoted to me than any retriever is to his master. She would come up to me in the field and rub her head against me, and plainly endeavour to introduce me to her son. But the son, then as now, would never quite surrender himself. Cinderella's devotion to me was complete. Warrior has always been devoted, but his devotion has been qualified by independence of judgment.

When Warrior was weaned he and his mother came back to Brooke, and for a time were turned out on "Sidling Paul," a famous field for horses. It was actually part of the identical land which Lord Harrington had chosen as the best place for the breeding establishment which the Government of this time thought of setting up.

It rises steeply, two hundred feet, from a wood, with a stream at each end, and is about a third of a mile in length. Jasper Morris, who looked after Warrior and his mother during these years, explained to me the other day:

"What I likes about 'Sidling Paul' is that she has water at each end so the colts be encouraged to walk first one way and then the other on the steep sides. That makes their legs strong, and their hearts big."

So Warrior had every advantage in his childhood. He lived in the ideal place. My readers will not find that hard to believe if they will look at the sketch that Munnings has made of it. It holds many exciting memories for me too, from the time when, as a small boy, I was always fearful of what strange terrors might lurk behind the deep-slotted windows of the barn, till the day of my first adventurous ride with Warrior beside the stream which runs softly through the meadow and down to the little Brooke church among the trees.

For that age-long problem, the breaking-in, was soon to come. Of course Warrior would come up to me, after his mother had greeted me affectionately, and snuff at me to make sure that I was the right man. Horses have an amazing scent, far more acute than dogs or any other animal that I know. He might then allow me to pat his neck, and run my hand down his forelegs, but any further advances he met with refusal.

So "Young Jim" came along, so clever at this strange business of accustoming man's greatest friend in the animal kingdom—his only real friend as I really think and quite frankly assert—to allowing himself to be ridden.

Cinderella inveigled her son into the stable yard at Brooke, and there a long conversation took place between Warrior, as he had already been named, and myself. A saddle was produced, and a bridle, and so back to "Sidling Paul."

"Young Jim" has very seldom been bucked off, but Warrior achieved that feat more often than all his other pupils put together. But in an amazingly short time Warrior liked being ridden by him.

By that time I was a Minister of the Crown and busy in London. One day, I got a letter from "Young Jim" telling me that he thought I ought to ride Warrior at once, so that I should be the first. How well I remember the adventure on "Sidling Paul!" "Young Jim" had wisely left me alone to my fate. An old groom, for some reason called by the strange name of "Henry Punch," was holding Warrior, now a fine two-year-old bay thoroughbred, with a white star on his forehead. He knew me very well, and whinnied as I walked up the path. I patted him on the neck, and, as so many thousands of people have done, tried to placate him with a lump of sugar. But he was very excited at meeting almost his first human friend armed with a riding crop, breeches and gaiters!

With deep respect I submit to those who know far more about horses than I do, that it is of the greatest importance to take your first ride on a horse that knows you, in just the same clothing, and, if you can manage it, just the same frame of mind as that in which you first talked to him as a tiny foal. Horses may not be so clever as human beings—even of that I am not sure—but one thing is certain, that they have far longer and more accurate memories. So always be the same to them, and, believe me, they will be the same to you.

However, I made this mistake myself the first time I rode Warrior. I put on special riding clothes, different from those in which I had talked to him so often before. Of course it seemed natural to me, but it was not natural to him. He snorted a little as I got on his back, and so, with much patting of his neck from me, and much encouragement, walked, ambled and trotted along the edge of "Sidling Paul." Sometimes he laid his ears back, till I talked to him and he put them forward again. But we went on quietly enough

A. J. Munnings

Sidling Paul

"SIDLING PAUL" HAS MANY EXCIT-
ING MEMORIES FOR ME. AS A SMALL
BOY I WAS ALWAYS FEARFUL OF
WHAT STRANGE TERRORS MIGHT
LURK BEHIND THE DEEP SLOTTED
WINDOWS OF THE BARN. WARRIOR
SPENT MUCH OF HIS EARLY LIFE
HERE AND IT WAS THE SCENE OF
OUR FIRST RIDE TOGETHER.

51

until we reached the little stream which runs through
that part of "Sidling Paul" called "Cow's Mead." We
had just arrived at the point where the stream runs
down between some ash trees when Warrior decided
that we must part!

Most people regard an episode of this kind as a contest between man and horse in which one or the other
must be victorious. Fortunately my Arab friend had
taught me the true lesson in the desert in 1895. He told
me that if you have infinite patience you can always
get control of any horse, but if you decide to win the
battle right away you may not succeed, and the
stronger animal may beat you in the long run.

My readers may have guessed that what I have just
written is a prelude to saying that Warrior bucked me
off three times over! But three times I managed to hold
on to him, and before I mounted the fourth time I had
a long talk with him. I remember so well sitting by
him on the slope of the steep hill with the ash trees
rustling overhead and the little Brooke stream trickling
beneath.

No horse understands the actual word that a man
says, he only appreciates the intonation of his voice.
I think I know what the horse does understand.
Scientists have shown that he understands anger by
placing an apparatus on his heart which proves that
an angry word from a man will increase its beat by
70 per cent., and, if accompanied by a menace, 100
per cent. Of course he understands the warning
word telling him to watch his steps. Of course he
understands the affectionate word, though so few

realise that it is the affectionate word he is waiting for all the time.

Well, I talked to Warrior under the ash tree, all alone with him and rather battered about by my successive falls. He looked at me, his nostrils distended, and I looked at him, trying to explain that I was a busy man, but that I loved him because I loved his mother, and would he please not buck me off any more, and if so we might be friends together for all our lives.

Those who read this book may think that what I write is fantastic and untrue, but I beg them to believe it is not. The gentle head was bent down to me as I talked, the nose was rubbed against my cheek, and from that moment to this, twenty-five years later, we have been constant comrades and friends, though I must confess that we have had our quarrels. Even the other day old Warrior shot me off his back as cleanly as he had done twenty years before because I wanted to go one way and he another. But directly he saw me on the ground he bent his neck, and, as previously, rubbed his head against me, and waited for me to jump on to his back.

In those twenty years we have had many adventures together, wonderful adventures, glorious adventures.

In the late War nearly all his comrades were killed, and nearly all of mine, but we both survived, and largely because of him. It is with a sense of duty that I write his story, the story of Warrior, my faithful friend, who never failed and never feared.

CHAPTER III

A CHARGER'S TRAINING

Warrior is introduced to the sea—Racehorse or charger?—In training at Burley-on-the-Hill with Major Hall—His friendship with Freddie Guest.

MY next adventure with Warrior as a two-year-old was introducing him to the sea.

I rode him down to the beach one lovely summer's morning, when only tiny waves were breaking on the shore. I had great difficulty in getting him to approach it; every time a little wave, less than a foot high, broke with a gentle murmur, Warrior pretended to be filled with mortal dread. I was leading him at this first lesson, hoping to ride him into the sea in due course. Twice in his pretended panics he broke away from me and galloped inland up the lifeboat road, but each time I caught him, and at last induced him to come right down to the edge of the water until it touched his feet. Then I sat down on the side of a boat which was ready to be launched for the lobster fishing, and gave him several lumps of sugar. Again he rubbed his head against my arm, saying quite clearly: "All right, all right; I understand this now. I will do anything you like."

I got on his back and rode him straight into the sea. He was so pleased with the cool water that he got out of his depth, and we both rolled over, I underneath him. By the time we had both got the right way up again I had decided it was time that this first lesson should come to an end.

Two years afterwards, not long before the War, when he was with me again, he would go down to the shore when there was a really heavy sea in winter time, and walk right to the bottom of the beach without flinching, although it has always seemed to me that a great breaking wave is a terrifying thing. He would follow the retreating water till the waves were breaking not more than ten yards from his nose, and then stand with feet well apart while the foamy water swept past his shoulders.

It was then that I first realised what an astonishingly courageous animal was mine, for I could see, though he trembled a little between my legs, that he was determined to overcome his fear.

I may perhaps give a word of warning to others who ride horses into the sea. When there are big waves sweeping back and forth again, perhaps twenty and thirty yards, it is very important that the horse's head should be straight on to the oncoming wave, or turned directly away from it. In other words, the horse's body must, except for the brief moment of turning, be at right angles to the beach and the line of the waves. It is not that if you let him stand broadside on the force of the waves knocks him down, but both he and you get giddy as the water sweeps away to seaward, and you gradually bend in the opposite direction until you both roll over sideways into the water.

But to return to Warrior's education. This had to be
completed, and "Young Jim," to Warrior's infinite
advantage and mine, took on the task. So back to
Yafford he went, and remained there for the next two
years, with no more than occasional visits to Brooke,
whenever I could be at home.

He was taught to be the perfect hack, to stand still
when mounted, to walk, trot, canter and gallop on
being given the spoken word. Then he was taught to
jump, and a wonderful jumper he became. He has
never refused anything with me, in peace or war,
except when he saw some hidden obstacle or difficulty,
which made the leap impossible of achievement without inviting disaster. But he would go straight—and
would still, I think, if I were unwise enough to ask
him—at five feet of unbreakable timber, or a six-foot
ditch with a stiff fence on the far side. All this "Young
Jim" taught him with infinite kindness and patience.
I do not know how often Warrior has been struck in
anger, but very, very seldom. I suppose that is the
reason why he is my companion and friend.

One day at the War Office, where I then was as War
Minister, my private secretary, who was getting used
to such interruptions, brought me a letter and said
with a smile: "Here is a question of far more importance than any other with which we are dealing." The
letter was from "Young Jim," and the problem was
whether to train Warrior as a racehorse or as a
charger. "Young Jim" pleaded that he might be a
racehorse, for he had discovered Warrior's remarkable
turn of speed. I said: "No; if he is constantly racing he

will never be a perfect charger; even his kindly nature will not stand the restraint of military exercises after the thrilling contests of the racecourse."

And so it was settled, to "Young Jim's" regret; but his view of Warrior's speed was confirmed in dramatic fashion just nine years later. After four years on the Western Front, a great part of the time pretty near the front line, where proper exercise was difficult, and, I suppose, everything was wanting to improve a horse's speed, and after four years of rest and little galloping after the War, "Young Jim" rode him to victory in the Isle of Wight Point-to-Point, on 30th March, 1922. It was the fourth anniversary of Warrior's greatest ordeal and mine, when Moreuil Ridge was re-captured, and thus the thrill of that wonderful day was all the greater.

But my decision in 1913 that Warrior must be a charger and not a racehorse involved his removal from Yafford and Brooke and his beloved Isle of Wight.

Captain Freddie Guest, of the 1st Life Guards, had a considerable establishment of horses at his Midland home, Burley-on-the-Hill. The man who looked after his horses for him was Major Hall, who had been riding master of the same distinguished regiment, and was, without doubt, one of the best horse masters of the day. He is fortunately still with us, and the other day wrote to me inquiring as to Warrior's welfare. I replied telling him that I had been begged to write the life of my old horse, and asking him if he could remember anything about him after the lapse of so many years.

Here is his answer:

"My recollections of Warrior, refreshed as it is by
some data, is: That he came to Burley-on-the-Hill
early in 1914, and left at the outbreak of War. A bay
or brown gelding of about 15·2 hands, 4 years old,
with a small intelligent head and a deep girth. His
training as a cavalry charger embraced the facing of
grotesque sights and rifle-fire. He also went through
the intricate figures of the musical ride, the rider
whistling a popular tune. Had Warrior received a
circus training he certainly would have become a
star performer, so great was his courage and placid
intelligence.

"On one summer's day General Seely and Captain
Guest were onlookers in the Park, when Warrior
displayed his keenness in giving them a show of his
skill.

" DOUGLAS HALL, *Hon. Major,*
" *Riding Master to the 1st Life Guards.*"

How well I remember that summer's morning in
1914! Another of the party was a great lover of horses,
F. E. Smith, afterwards Lord Birkenhead. Major
Hall rode Warrior himself, and showed us his
numerous accomplishments. He told us he was
much attached to my horse, as indeed was everyone
else. Freddie Guest said to me: "Yes, he is one of the
most lovable horses I have ever had to do with."
Warrior was overjoyed to see me again after six months'
separation, and trotted up to me neighing loudly, and

rubbed his head against my shoulder, as has been his custom since his birth.

Freddie Guest, "F. E.," Warrior and I were to meet in very different surroundings within a few months of that day.

Freddie Guest writes to me:

"Herewith a few notes from Major Hall and myself relating to Warrior's early days. I do not remember much about the time when he was with me at G.H.Q. in 1914, except that I think I rode him the day of the Battle of Le Cateau. I remember the Field Marshal deciding on the line which, in his opinion, should be held during the retreat. It was a wonderful September day and the stubble fields were full of partridges and hares. It may be that this was the first time that he ever saw a battlefield.

"He went to the War with uncanny wisdom, seeming to know that he had a part to play in human affairs. He brought his master safely home from four years of shot and shell."

And here I must record that Warrior's best friend, apart from "Young Jim" and myself, has been Freddie Guest. He trained him and cared for him, and took him to the War. When my duties took me to the French and Belgian fronts during these hard and bitter days of defeat, it was Freddie who looked after Warrior, rode him whenever he could, and kept him alive when so many hundreds of horses perished from exhaustion and hunger.

"F. E." was to meet Warrior in the grim and gloomy
swamps where the Indian troops found themselves, in
water-logged trenches in Northern France, in the
winter of 1914. Indeed, Warrior was in "F. E.'s"
charge for a brief period just behind the front line
during that melancholy time, while I was being des-
patched to the French front. On Warrior's behalf
I thank Freddie and " F. E."—his devoted friends.

CHAPTER IV

WARRIOR GOES TO WAR

The decision—Warrior meets the French—Making the bridge jump at Compiègne—A narrow escape in the Retreat—His first experience of shell-fire.

ON the 5th of August, 1914, I met Freddie Guest in the House of Commons. He said to me:

"Well, we shall be starting for this war, you and I, in the next few days. What shall I do with your Warrior?"

I asked him whether he was not too young for the very strenuous life which any horse had to endure out there.

I remember so well his reply:

"Well, we decided weeks ago that we would throw everything into this war, in addition to our obvious duty as officers in the Reserve to go there ourselves. Our motor-cars are going, anything else that can be useful, and as many of those who have been with us in any capacity as are fit and ready to come, our grooms, our chauffeurs; you tell me all your children too as they get old enough. Surely it would be a shame to leave Warrior behind? He would hate it, and, besides, Hall tells me that he has a wonderful constitution. He has never been sick or sorry all the time he has been with us."

61

So I gladly consented, and Warrior and I moved at once to Southampton to be embarked for France.

By great good fortune we crossed in the same boat and walked ashore together. I thought from the first that we were in for a long war, but I did not think that we should be in that country together for more than four years, nor did I dare to hope that if that should be our fate, we should both return alive.

It was indeed extraordinary that Warrior returned safely, as the story of his time in France will show. Some people have said that I was the luckiest man on the Western Front. I do not think I can claim that quaint distinction, but I am sure that, as far as horses go, Warrior can. There are thousands of the Canadians, with whom he served for more than three years, who will endorse this verdict. I often heard them say: "The bullet hasn't been made that can hurt Warrior." He really did bear a charmed life.

From Havre, where we landed, Warrior went on by train; I was ahead in a motor-car making for Le Cateau. Sir John French, commanding the Expeditionary Force, was to have his headquarters there when he arrived.

Von Kluck's advancing host was still far away, and all the talk was of our victorious advance with the French on our right, and the Belgians on our left. I had much to do as the special service officer of the Expeditionary Force, but every moment I could spare from long motor drives to the east or north, I would spend riding about the countryside with Warrior—the best form of relaxation.

How well Warrior must remember the cheers and waving of little Union Jacks from all the people, the women and the old men, as we rode through the long street of Le Cateau, or through the villages nearby. The whole population was in a frenzy of joy at our arrival. There were shouts of "Vivent les Anglais," "à Berlin," "notre Alsace," and "notre Lorraine." Warrior would arch his neck and paw the ground, while I was asking some local inhabitant, generally a very old man, or perhaps some pretty girl, what they had heard of the progress of events.

They were all quite certain of victory. There was not one of those poor creatures who was not firmly convinced that now, at last, proud Germany's pretensions would be set at nought, and that, thereafter, universal peace would reign. But very soon enthusiasm waned as the ominous rumours reached Le Cateau of the fall of Liège, and the German advance through Belgium.

I was sent forward to Mauberge, and Warrior was left for Freddie to ride. He has described to me the day when he rode past Le Cateau, with the civilians feverishly digging trenches while a few ricochet bullets hummed over, and crashing shells began to fall.

The British Headquarters had already been moved twenty miles nearer to Paris so as to direct Haig's and Smith-Dorrien's retiring columns while Freddie Guest, on Warrior, and Sir John French were still surveying the battle on horseback, and ruefully making up their minds that because of that swift encircling movement they must complete the retirement at maximum speed.

All through that disastrous retreat I saw Warrior from time to time, but seldom had a chance to ride him, for most of the time my duties were with the rearguard, sending constant messages by motor-cyclist of the position of the retiring troops.

But one day during the retreat, when we happened to meet, Warrior had a very narrow escape from capture or death.

British Headquarters were at Compiègne, where I arrived early one morning from the French front to make my report to Sir John French. Next morning the retirement of the English and French forces continued, and Headquarters had to be moved farther south towards Paris.

Henry Wilson said to me: "The French have told me that the great bridge is mined, and that at the right moment they will 'make it jump.' *Faire sauter* they call it. Now we want to get all our men across. Your duties will be to stay behind with our own engineers and the French officer in charge of the demolition, and ask him to delay until the last minute."

I asked if it really would be "made to jump."

"That I rather doubt," he answered, "it's a big bridge, but they tell me it has been scientifically mined."

Off I went in a motor-car to the bridge and found the demolition party and the French officer. We waited there while many of our troops crossed, until a motor-cyclist came dashing up with a message to say that a large number of the German cavalry had swum the river about three miles upstream, and were advancing on Paris. Presently we heard the sound of rifle-fire, apparently some two miles distant on the south side of the river.

The French officer said to me: "We must make the bridge jump now, or we shall be too late."

I had to agree, the button was pressed, and there was a tremendous roar as half the bridge went up; but enough of it remained to allow the passage of infantry and cavalry. By this time the sound of rifle-fire was nearer, but not much nearer.

The French officer said: "Now I will make the rest to jump."

With incredible zeal and energy he and his men, and our sappers, laid fresh charges on the girders, hoping they might do more damage, though they were unlikely to destroy the whole structure. However, we made a glorious bang, and though much of the bridge remained, it was quite clear it would prevent the passage of guns.

Then all of us started to ride back in lorries and motor-cars which had been waiting for the purpose. The rest of the party went some way downstream, but I steered due south by a little lane that I had noticed on the map. Freddie Guest had told me early that morning that this would be the best line of retreat. It was a narrow lane, but the surface was good, which was lucky for me, because the Germans had got almost to this point, and I had to pass through a regular fusillade of fire.

65

About three miles farther on I saw two lorries on the
road, one with its wheel off, while men were working
hard to take the load out of the broken lorry, and put
it on the sound one. In charge of the operations was
Freddie Guest. The rifle-fire got nearer and nearer,
but we got the boxes containing the more important
papers into the sound lorry, and were about to set
fire to the remainder, when the bullets began to
hum over.

At this moment who should appear but Warrior,
ridden by my groom, Thomson. Thomson was quite
unperturbed, and, in fact, seemed half asleep.

"For God's sake," I said, "get along, and join
Headquarters."

He replied: "I don't know where Headquarters
are."

I remember patting Warrior, who was trembling a
little at the sound of rifle-fire, and the hum of bullets
going over his head.

"Do you see the sun?" (It was about one o'clock.)
"Now gallop for one hour straight at it, without
stopping, and then begin to inquire where General
Headquarters are likely to be."

I gave Warrior a pat, and off they went at a full
gallop. Then Freddie Guest and I got into the motor-
car, and with the sound lorry proceeded on our way.
But Warrior went much faster than we did, and
fetched up safely at Sir John French's new headquarters long before we arrived.

Forty-eight hours later, Warrior and I were again
together on that sunny summer's day when Von

Kluck's advance had succeeded beyond his own wildest dreams, and the way to Paris lay open to him. We had a strong rearguard covering Dammartin. It was there, returned from the French front, that I found my faithful servant, Smith, and Warrior. We were all very sad, for it seemed even to the most stout-hearted folk that we had lost the War. But I got on Warrior's back, and cantered out towards the left flank of the rearguard. I knew that though doom impended, the opposing infantry were still eight miles away, and that I could best follow my instructions by going to the rearguard with my horse.

It was early morning on about the 30th of August. "Bend Or," as we called the Duke of Westminster, who was one of the headquarters staff and showed me constant kindness, had given me breakfast. Warrior was fit and well and we galloped north-east through smiling country. I patted Warrior's neck, and he whinnied in reply. Well, well, I thought, come what may, he and I would see the War through together; and strange though it may seem, for a few brief moments I was completely happy. But, of course, it could not last. We rode into a small village, where some of our men were posted, and so to the little château where the mayor lived. As I talked to him, and gave him certain information which I had been told to convey, we heard the crashing roar of shells. The stables of the château were hit, and immediately burst into flames.

It was the first time that I had ridden Warrior under shell-fire. I said good-bye to the mayor, mounted Warrior, who was standing outside, and rode out through the little gate past the blazing stables. As we approached them another bouquet of shells fell and burst, the nearest only a few yards away. To my amazement Warrior made no attempt to run away. I could feel him tremble a little between my legs as we trotted through the gate, but he pretended to be quite unperturbed. He was trying to be brave, and succeeding in his task.

On many, many days thereafter, during the four years that were to follow, I rode Warrior in shell-fire—sometimes so heavy that he was almost the only survivor—but never once did he attempt to bolt or do any of the things which might be expected of an animal reputed to be so naturally timid as the horse. No, my stout-hearted horse not only kept his own fear under control, but by his example helped beyond measure his rider and his friend to do the same.

CHAPTER V

FROM THE MARNE TO THE AISNE

Warrior advances again—Another narrow escape—His friend Sir John French—Safety in movement—Warrior becomes an old hand at war—But always dislikes rifle-fire—He takes part in the First Battle of Ypres—Racing the aeroplanes.

AFTER those brief and strangely happy hours near Dammartin, the melancholy retreat continued. I sent Warrior back to rejoin Freddie Guest with the Headquarters horses while I stayed behind to report on the situation of the ultimate rearguard.

For two dreadful days all seemed lost. The French Government had gone to Bordeaux, our wonderful little expeditionary force was reduced to less than half its numbers, the German advance continued with relentless steps. Then came the greatest relief in my experience. It was rightly termed "the crowning mercy" of the Marne. All the world knows that Von Kluck was ordered to turn to his left instead of entering Paris as he could have done; the French attacked with really fanatical valour, the Germans fought back with equal bravery, and our little army bore its part. I like to think, as every Englishman must do, that the balance was so uncertain on those fateful days that it well may be that we English turned the scale.

Warrior was with me during our advance to the Marne. Those who have not been brought up with horses, especially with Arab horses, will think that I attribute undue intelligence to him on this and so many other occasions, but I ask them to believe me when I recount that, weary as he was—he had been retreating south and west for ten terrible days—my young horse became a totally new creature when we turned about and marched towards the morning sun.

Gaily we rode forward. Exhausted German soldiers, cut off by the French army's swift advance, were surrendering in great numbers on all sides. There was nothing else for them to do, brave men as they were. Many parties that I met had lost all their officers. But they were stout-hearted men, and, as time went on, Warrior and I, and the Canadian soldiers with whom we served for the rest of the War, learnt more and more to admire their tenacity and courage.

The advance of our armies was held up for a time at Ferté-sous-Jouarre, but, in the end, we got through, and crossed the bridge. Both Warrior and I nearly finished our careers at Ferté-sous-Jouarre. Warrior was with a bunch of horses in the midst of which a big shell fell. He was one of a few survivors. I was sent down into the village, and ran forward with a sergeant and eight men of the Lancashire Regiment. Our party was caught by accurate machine-gun fire, and every one of the party was laid stone dead except myself. Warrior was about three hundred yards from me when this happened.

And so forward to the Aisne, where the Germans

had prepared a defensive position which we proposed to storm, and continue our victorious advance.

Sir John French's Headquarters were established at Fère-en-Tardenois, where I rejoined Warrior after the mêlée in Ferté-sous-Jouarre. Sir John French frequently rode him at this time, while I would have one of Freddie Guest's horses. French loved to reconnoitre a position on horseback, saying, quite truthfully, that although you are a bigger mark on a horse, you are ten times less likely to be hit as you gallop forward or to the flank, if you are spotted, and fired on. I followed this rule myself all through the War, even when I was living, as I did for so long, in a battalion headquarters. Swift movement is worth any amount of protection.

French was a very fine horseman, and loved and understood horses. He and Warrior got on very well together, and thus began a friendship which was to prove invaluable during the First Battle of Ypres, as I shall presently tell.

During the few days that I was at Fère-en-Tardenois I saw much of Warrior, and was thrilled to find how clever he was becoming at this war business. He no longer trembled at the burst of a shell, unless it was rather near, but even then it was only a quiver. He had quite clearly come to the conclusion that one ought not to shrink from shell-fire. Those who are good enough to read to the end of this book will see that this remarkable horse ultimately overcame all fear of it, however near, and that although for years he was always concerned at rifle-fire, at the supreme moment of his life and mine, he completely overcame his dread of even that most unnerving of all dangers.

But very soon I had to hand him over once more to the care of his devoted friend, Freddie Guest, Sir John French's chief aide-de-camp, while I was sent off to represent the Commander-in-Chief at Antwerp. Antwerp was an exciting place just then, but, for once in my life, I was rather glad that Warrior was not with me, for I could never have got him across the Scheldt. The bridge would not have borne him when I crossed, and he could hardly have swum that broad river unaided. But we rejoined each other at Bailleuil, on the borders of Belgium, before long.

While I had been away at Antwerp the British army had made a flank march from the Aisne to Hazebrouck, and thence to Ypres, driving the German rearguard before them. Sir John French's main headquarters had been established at St. Omer, but he pushed forward an advance headquarters to Bailleuil as soon as that little town was clear of the enemy. There he kept his horses. Freddie Guest and his other aide-de-camp, Fitz Watt, made all arrangements. The arrangements included Warrior.

I remember kissing the old boy on the nose when I saw him in his rather battered stable some days after we returned from Antwerp, but I was not to have much time for riding him. The British army was covering Armentières and Ypres, the French army joining with them north of Ypres up to and including Dixmüde. Next to them was the remainder of the gallant little Belgian army, commanded by King

Albert in person, and stretching almost up to the North Sea. Then, on the extreme left of the long line from Switzerland to the North Sea, and protecting a vital point at Nieupoort, came a portion of the French army, commanded by General Dimitri.

My duty was to visit each of these little army groups each day, and report back to Sir John French. It was known that the Germans were advancing in great force; in fact, they had already got their 17-inch guns, which they had brought up from Antwerp, into a position from which they could shell both Dixmüde and Ypres. The First Battle of Ypres was impending.

I have often thought that those who have written about the early phases of the World War have missed the true point about the action of the British army in France and Flanders. They have magnified the Retreat from Mons and have not paid enough attention to the First Battle of Ypres. Many acts of self-sacrificing valour were performed during the retreat from Mons, and some of them I witnessed with Warrior. But a considerable part of the army had no chance to fight ; the swift encircling movement of Von Kluck's army meant still swifter retirement by our troops in order to avoid being cut off and captured. On the other hand, at the First Battle of Ypres, when the British army, reinforced with a few battalions of the Territorial Force, found themselves confronted by four times their numbers of most courageous men, with an overwhelming superiority of artillery gathered from all parts of their long battle line in France, then every man, from general to private soldier, and every horse, had to

73

play his part. It was a wonderful battle. I did not know before that men could be so self-sacrificing and so brave. They all knew that if they failed, and the Channel ports were captured, it was all over with the Allied cause, and, perhaps, with England too. So they fought for weeks on end in blood, and mud, and misery with a spirit never equalled in the history of the British army. I love to know that my Warrior bore his humble part in that august event.

French was the life and soul of the defence. It is his true title to fame. Whenever and wherever things were most desperate, then and there would he be on horseback, encouraging his weary men forward to take the place of those who had fallen, with cheery words, and occasional little speeches, as he rode along with them. Often Warrior was the horse he rode.

But at last the desperate Battle of Ypres died down, and Warrior had a rest from war's alarms. He went back to St. Omer, many miles behind the front line, and found himself doing nothing more dramatic or exciting than carrying the Commander-in-Chief, or one of his staff, on a quiet ride, including on most days an inspection of the troops arriving from England, or of those withdrawn from the front line for a rest.

From there I was sent to report on the front held by the Indian contingent, and took Warrior with me. It was the wettest and gloomiest part of the line, and rifle-fire was continuous. Each side wanted to find out what the other was worth, so once again Warrior found himself exposed to that dangerous thing, "rifle-and machine-gun fire."

Then a bit of good luck befell him. He got a bad attack of internal cramp, and was taken back to G.H.Q. at St. Omer. The very next day I rode up to the front line with F. E. Smith, and both the horses we rode were wounded. When I got back to St. Omer Warrior had quite recovered. Christmas was approaching, too, and a kind of informal armistice prevailed along most of the front.

I had a week's holiday before going to the French front, and during that time rode Warrior every day. One game that he greatly enjoyed was racing the aeroplanes that took off from the aerodrome on the hill above the little town. The pilot would be ready, and bets were made as to who would be leading at a given point at the far end of the aerodrome. Of course Warrior could jump off so quickly that within a few paces he was travelling at twenty-five miles an hour, while the aeroplane took some seconds to gather way. The point chosen for the finish of the race, by which time the aeroplane was well in the air, was so well devised by the commanding officer, himself a lover of horses, and, of course, of Warrior—the most lovable horse of all—that we often achieved a dead heat. But, looking back on this one week of holiday, I cannot but be filled with wonder that so highly-strung a creature as a horse, with ultra-sensitive nerves and sense of hearing, should have rejoiced in a contest which meant that for quite a minute he was exposed to the full roar of an unsilenced aeroplane engine.

Here again, quite clearly, this strange creature was

preparing himself for every ordeal. He must have hated the roar, but he thought it was all part of the curious game that he was playing, in which he had to learn to endure everything most hateful to him. For, see already to what he had been exposed—violent noise, the bursting of great shells (this he had already learnt to bear although so hateful to his acute ear), and bright flashes at night, when the white light of bursting shells must have caused violent pain to such sensitive eyes as horses possess. Above all, there was the smell of blood, terrifying to every horse. Many people do not realise how acute is his sense of smell, but most of them will have read of his terror when he smells blood. Warrior had been through all these ordeals, and had steeled himself to bear them. So the minor ordeal of racing an aeroplane was something which he could almost enjoy.

CHAPTER VI

WARRIOR MEETS THE CANADIANS

Back to England—Warrior meets the Canadians—And wins their affection—"Here comes old Warrior"—His second landing in France— His remarkable escape in the Ypres Salient—But he waits for his master—He learns to follow like a dog—A lapse of etiquette—Escape from a burning stable.

SOON after the New Year of 1915 I received a summons to report myself to Lord Kitchener at the War Office. I asked Sir John French if I could take Warrior with me to England.

His answer was, " Certainly; I owe much to your young horse. As long as I am Commander-in-Chief, wherever you go, he shall go too."

So to England we went together, Warrior to Brooke, to meet his mother, Cinderella, once more, and I to the War Office, to see Lord Kitchener. There I received the news that I was to command all the available Canadian cavalry, to be formed into a mounted brigade, three thousand men and horses, comprising cavalry, artillery, engineers, signallers and army service corps, a wonderful command for any man to be privileged to lead. And such men. The flower of the youth of Canada, with soldiers already famous to lead them, such men as Archie Macdonnell commanding Lord Strathcona's

Horse, who had already led the Canadian North-West Mounted Police in many great adventures in the remotest parts of the Canadian frontier.

Lord Kitchener devoted far more time than he should have done, in view of his great responsibilities as Secretary of State, to the details of forming the little force which I was to command. But I am correspondingly grateful to his memory.

I telegraphed for Warrior to join me at Salisbury, and there found him with his groom, Thomson, and my servant, Smith. Thence we set out to find our new comrades, men and horses, destined to serve together for nearly the whole of the rest of the War.

And here may I make a frank confession, and beg my readers to believe that it is true. I never could have earned the love and affection which was granted to me but for Warrior. Thousands of Canadians now living will confirm this fact. This handsome, gay, bay thoroughbred, with the white star on his forehead, was my passport wherever I went. As time went on, especially in France, where we soon returned, the men got to love him more and more. As I rode along, whether it were in rest billets, in reserve, approaching the line, or in the midst of battle, men would say, not "Here comes the General," but "Here's old Warrior."

It amused me again the other day while I was in the middle of writing this book, just nineteen years later, to hear some boy scouts, whom I went to visit in camp, shout out without any reference to me as I rode up, the same cry—"Here comes old Warrior."

It is a most mysterious thing that this old horse, like some great personality among men, impresses himself upon all whenever he appears; walking about a field by himself, or at any other moment, all eyes turn to look at him. I do not know why, but so it is, and so it was with Warrior when he first met the Canadian cavalry, the artillery and the engineers.

It was a new life for him. He had experienced for many months the shocks and excitements of modern war, and had learnt to control himself at terrifying moments, but he had always been a member of a small and select party—the horses attached to General Headquarters. Now he met some thousands of his own kind, and had to be one of them. He rose to the occasion, and made friends with them all, unless, I am bound to add, one of them should prove unduly familiar or quarrelsome. He earned the respect and, indeed, the affection of all of them.

While this remarkable unit was being finally assembled and welded into one in England, came the news of the first gas attack of the World War during the Second Battle of Ypres. Reinforcements were urgently needed, and again I was summoned to the War Office to see Lord Kitchener.

He asked me: "Will you take your command to Flanders at once, leaving all your horses behind? I make one condition if you say 'yes,' as I know you will. The men themselves must volunteer to go without their horses. I know how much they love them, and I do not think it fair to order them against their will to go without them."

I said: "You need not ask that question. Of course every man will volunteer in this emergency."

"That may be," he replied, "but I must ask you to go back to them, and ask them to volunteer."

The whole proceeding struck me as strange, but I daresay Kitchener was right.

Anyway, when I rejoined my men I summoned my commanding officers, and told them what Lord Kitchener had said. They answered me that of course every man would go, much as they loved the horses which they had brought from Canada with them, and that the question need not be asked. However, I told them to carry out the Secretary of State's instructions.

Every man came forward without hesitation, and off we went to France within twenty-four hours, leaving the horses behind, all except the horses of the commanding officers, and, of course, Warrior, who walked on to the ship with me, and with the utmost self-possession ensconced himself in a quiet place in the alleyway.

It was a rough passage, in the dark, and I spent most of the time talking to Warrior, and giving him corn. I well remember our arrival at Boulogne at six o'clock on a spring morning. I led Warrior first off the gangway, and got on his back on the railway line, sitting there as the men filed off. As they formed up somebody shouted out: " Three cheers for Warrior." The unexpected shout disconcerted him, and I thought for a moment we were both going over the dock wall. But not at all; as always, he kept his head; and so we proceeded to the front, where we were soon involved in a desperate battle.

This time Warrior had not got all the advantages of being " attached to General Headquarters." On the contrary, he found himself tethered behind a little haystack into which shells and long-range bullets would thud from time to time. But he had indeed become war-worthy. He did not flinch or tremble, though the din of battle was deafening, and when darkness fell, and I mounted him to ride round the lines, he was cool and self-possessed.

When the fighting died down at Festubert we moved north to take over a sector of the line just south of the Ypres Salient. Here Warrior had a real stable under Hill 63. True, it had holes in the roof and no windows, but it boasted a manger and a hay-rack, and he obviously enjoyed returning to something approaching civilisation.

In order to reach the front line we had to go over a ridge which should have been in full view of the enemy, but a row of trees actually screened one from view. Consequently, as the Germans could not be shooting all the time, it was a fairly safe business going into the front line in daylight. It was all the more safe if we rode there, because we covered the distance in about one quarter the time, and were therefore four times more likely to come off unscathed.

Living in all sorts of uncomfortable places was, of course, one of the ordeals which Warrior, and every other horse, had to go through in France. Sometimes he was comparatively lucky and found himself with

81

some sort of a roof over his head like the one that Munnings has painted. But this was a palace compared with some of the places where he was stabled; more often his only shelter consisted of a tarpaulin stretched across a wire in a muddy trench or behind a sodden haystack.

For several weeks in the summer of 1915 Warrior and I would gallop over this ridge, and down into the valley below, where ran the support line. We did this at some time every day and generally again at night. I should think it must have been about the fortieth time that Warrior had gone to this spot so near to the enemy front line—I suppose about six hundred yards at the nearest point—that he had a most unnerving experience and behaved with extraordinary courage.

The hot summer had withered the leaves on some of the trees, and the concussion of bursting shells, of which there were many in this sector, had shaken them off. No doubt the German forward observing officer of one of the nearer batteries spotted the horses while I was away in the front line with my brigade major. We had left Warrior and the other horse in the charge of an orderly from one of the nearby squadron headquarters.

While I was walking along the front line behind the parapet, a salvo of shells came over and fell with a roar a few hundred yards behind us.

I said to my companion: "That's uncommon near to our horses," but we had to go on attending to our business. Then came two more shells directed to about

THIS RUINED BARN WAS A PALACE
COMPARED WITH SOME OF THE
PLACES WHERE WARRIOR WAS
STABLED IN FRANCE.

83

the same spot and then silence. It must have been about an hour and a half later when we returned by another communication trench to the point where we had left them.

A strange thing had happened. One of the German shells, instead of bursting into small fragments when it struck the ground, had broken in half, as they sometimes did. One half of the shell had struck my brigade major's horse straight in the chest, and cut it clean in half. The orderly was knocked down by the force of the blow, and must have been unconscious for a little time. He was still sitting on the ground when we returned, and there was Warrior, who had just moved away a few yards, and was waiting for me. He neighed loudly as I came in sight, and cantered up to me, saying quite clearly: "I would not leave you."

Now be it observed that the horse knew his way back perfectly well, and many shells had dropped quite near after the one that had cut the horse alongside of him in half. He knew that all he had to do was to gallop over the hill back to his stable and comparative safety; but he would not, although the man was lying on the ground and the other horse was dead.

It was during this period that Warrior took to following me about like a dog, without saddle or bridle, when I was riding a pony that I had called Patrick. Part of the force was in the front line, and another part in immediate reserve about two miles behind, and I made it a rule to ride around and see those in reserve each day, before or after going into the front line.

One day Warrior broke out of his stable when I was starting off, and followed me. The men wanted to catch him, but I dissuaded them. For weeks thereafter, and, indeed, all through that summer, Warrior would follow me, whether I was mounted or on foot, wherever I went.

This eccentric proceeding was without incident except when I rode out to meet two batteries of horse artillery which, although forming part of my command, had been detached from me for some weeks. On my pony Patrick I rode up to the commanding officer, Colonel (now General) Panet, to greet him, followed by Warrior. But when Warrior saw his old friends of the horse artillery he was filled with glee. He whinnied at the Colonel's horse, had a playful kick at the second-in-command's, cantered up to one of the leading gun teams, and when scared away by the crack of a whip, galloped round and round in transports of joy till he finally got his feet into a little ditch, turned over on his back and was left with his legs sticking up in the air! However, he soon extricated himself, and from that moment onwards was always perfectly demure and self-possessed.

Unfortunately our comfortable headquarters at Petit Douve Farm were smashed up and burnt to ashes by German artillery fire towards the end of our stay. Warrior was out grazing at the time, and surveyed the burning of his home with interest, but without alarm.

So I had to transport my headquarters elsewhere. I found a nice farm on the *pavé* road that runs from Neuve Eglise towards Lille. Here we were a little farther from the front line, but this time in full view of it. I reasoned that the Germans had left this farm untouched, and would continue to do so, because they might want to occupy it when they advanced; for a fortnight the theory worked perfectly.

Here Warrior had a really good stable with a door facing towards the Germans. I was asleep one morning when my aide-de-camp woke me with a shout saying that the house was on fire, and had already been hit about six times!

I jumped up in pyjamas and with bare feet, and ran across the yard to Warrior's stable. I would not dare to recount this episode but that there are many eye-witnesses living who will confirm it. I could hear Warrior beating against the door with his forefeet. I threw it open and out he bounded. I ran after him to catch his headstall, and before I had gone two yards a shell burst right inside his stable, and knocked the whole place to smithereens. It was a miraculously lucky escape.

As winter came on we all had a harder time. It was a very wet season, the ground was soggy, trenches were filled with water, and in riding about the country we were constantly getting bogged.

But it was, nevertheless, at this time, and in both succeeding winters on the Western Front, that we learnt that the horse is the only certain means of transport. The horse is vital to man in modern

THIS BILLET OF WARRIOR'S REALLY
LOOKS LIKE A PALACE; ACTUALLY IT
IS ALL THAT WAS LEFT OF A SUGAR
FACTORY AFTER AN INTENSE GER-
MAN BOMBARDMENT — PERHAPS
WARRIOR'S MOST UNCOMFORTABLE
AND HAZARDOUS HOME.

war. All mechanical contrivances fail when the mud gets deep; the horse suffers, but some survive to pull up the batteries, to bring up food and ammunition, to drag back the long melancholy lines of ambulances.

CHAPTER VII

BEHIND THE LINE

Akbar, a new friend—Warrior eats his stable—He rejoins an old friend, Prince Antoine of Orleans—Horses and dogs—The Battle of the Somme—A chance for the cavalry—Disappointment—How Warrior nearly died.

AT last respite came from blood and mud. After eight months spent nearly continuously in the trenches, news came, to the infinite joy of my men, that we were to be reformed as a mounted brigade, with a view to our being employed in moving warfare. I believe at the time the intention was that we should go to Palestine. So back we went to the quiet French countryside, almost out of sound of the shells, to find the whole of our horses returned to us.

Warrior remembered many of them, but he found a great new friend, who was to be his companion for close on fifteen years. This was a little thoroughbred Arab, of a rather wild disposition, which my son Frank brought with him when he joined me as A.D.C. Akbar was a very dark bay, with two black and two white feet; moreover he had a large white blaze on his forehead, which reached to one eye, so he looked at you with one brown eye and one white one, which gave his face a rather comical appearance. Warrior and he became quite inseparable, and during the two

HERE IS A VIVID STUDY BY MUNNINGS OF THE
CANADIAN CAVALRY MOVING FORWARD IN THE
DEVASTATED AREA.

90

91

and a half years of war that followed, they were never parted except for a short time when Akbar and I were wounded.

Warrior's affection for me and Akbar had its embarrassing side also. If put in one of the little French stables made of wattle and daub he would eat his way out! But when he did get out he would come straight to wherever I was. We only cured the trouble by putting him in the more substantial stable of an old French château where I also found a lodging.

Here we were joined by a man who turned out to be one of Warrior's best friends, Prince Antoine of Orleans, a son of the Comte d'Eu and a distant cousin of our own King. He was in the Austrian cavalry before the War, and was a fine rider and a great lover of horses. As he was debarred by law from serving in the French army he joined the British army by special permission of the King, on the first day of the War, and was with me at Le Cateau and during the Retreat. Then he went to the 2nd Army for more than a year, returning to me when we were reformed as a mounted brigade, as assistant aide-de-camp. He brought a good horse with him, but was pleased to renew his previous acquaintance with Warrior.

If you happen to be a General you will note with what immense interest your horse will eye the new A.D.C. He knows very well that much of his comfort and well-being depends on this mysterious man who always goes about with his master, and seems able to order about people who are much older than

A FAMILIAR SCENE WITH THE
CANADIAN CAVALRY. OFFICERS'
HORSES WATERING NEAR BERNE-
VILLE.

93

himself! Horses are even quicker than dogs at noticing these things, although, unlike dogs, they are not snobs. The unattached dog will always attach himself to the senior man of any party. I have seen a dog join up with a private soldier, then in a day or two transfer his attentions to the sergeant. Within a week he is walking along with the company commander with a proud air of proprietorship, and only an occasional patronising look for the private and the sergeant. Horses, on the other hand, are no respecters of persons, or at least of rank. Warrior was just as fond of my servant, Smith, as he was of me, and so I think he is still.

But to return to Warrior's stay at the château. It was certainly his happiest time during the War, except for that brief glorious moment of victory on 30th March, 1918. Not only was he well groomed and fed, not only were there no muddy trenches and no barbed wire, but we were quite near the sea. It was wonderful to see him the first day I rode him down to the beach. He galloped straight into the sea up to his belly, and greatly wanted to lie down and roll in the cool water. So I rode him out again and took off his saddle and bridle, and in he went, followed by Akbar. They played together in the water like a couple of happy children.

But our period of resting and refitting did not last very long. We moved up, three thousand men and horses with our two batteries of artillery, and our own transport and signals and engineers, to a place not far from St. Pol. It was there that Warrior and I first saw a tank, then a great secret and carefully guarded. He soon got accustomed to these monstrous things, which was just as well, for he was to have a good deal to do with them later on in the War.

We practised all kinds of manœuvres, the idea being that the infantry were to break the German front line, and that the cavalry were then to sweep through the gap and take the enemy in the rear. It was my mounted brigade that was selected to lead this attack. I am afraid that not many of us who had spent a long time in the trenches, thought that the infantry could break through, or at any rate not until a great force of tanks had been assembled. However, we all played up to the part, and did our utmost to get our horses as fit as possible, and well accustomed to machine-gun and rifle-fire. Here Warrior's absolutely fearless nature was a great advantage. He set an example to all the other horses.

Then came the memorable day of the 1st of July, the opening of the Battle of the Somme.

The bombardment on our side was intense. My whole force was assembled in a slight hollow about twelve hundred yards behind the front line. Warrior and I, with Frank and Antoine and a single squadron, were four hundred yards farther forward. A battery of 18-pounders was just behind us, and the noise of the guns firing almost straight over our heads was terrific, but I noticed that Warrior, whom I was holding by the bridle as I lay on the ground, did not mind in the least after getting over the shock of the first shot.

We were just to the right of Fricourt, and our infantry in this sector made a considerable advance, although it may be remembered that on the left no advance was found possible. When I received a message that the infantry had taken two lines of trenches I jumped on to Warrior, and with my son, my second horse, Bazentin, my A.D.C.'s and one troop, rode forward and down into the next valley ahead of us. The infantry had just taken the crest of the hill in front. As we cantered up the side of the valley the infantry in support cheered us to the echo, thinking that this was the beginning of the "great break through." A shell dropped in the middle of us, and killed one of the orderlies' horses just behind me. Bazentin was wounded in the off foreleg and Antoine's horse in the neck, but both kept going.

When we got to the foot of the ridge we found that the infantry were completely held up, and that no further advance would be possible, at any rate for that day. I sent back a message to my second-in-command to this effect, and the rest of us waited where we were for a bit to make quite sure. But it became quite clear that there was no hope whatever of a further advance, and regretfully we had to gallop back. We had suffered few casualties in men and horses, but we were sorely disappointed to have been of so little service. Bazentin recovered from his wound after a few weeks, but Antoine's horse died. Warrior was waiting for me unhurt when we returned.

During the first few weeks of the battle we remained constantly in readiness, and I would ride Warrior every day up to the front line to see how matters progressed. One day he was lame, and I rode another horse, a chestnut; a chance shell hit him and killed him. I had three ribs broken myself, although I did not know it, but my first thought was: "What luck it was not Warrior!"

But after a while it became clear that cavalry could not be employed, and in our case the horses were sent back far behind the lines with some of the men. The rest of us resumed our places with the infantry. I kept Warrior with me, and at Bray-sur-Somme, behind the front line, he nearly met his end.

I had asked two French officers, who were going to lead an attack on the following night, to dine with me in the ruin where my headquarters were. My servant rushed in about midnight saying: "There is something wrong with Warrior."

I ran out to the remnant of a stable where Warrior was living. It was pitch dark, but Thomson was there with a lantern.

Anyone who has never seen a powerful thoroughbred suffering agonies from internal pain can have no conception of the terrible sight. The energy of those wonderful muscles, which enable him to gallop at thirty miles an hour and jump six feet in the air, is used in the most fantastic and fearful contortions in the endeavour to dislodge the cause of the pain. Warrior was leaping about in this battered loose-box like a mad thing, hurling himself into the air, falling on to his back, jumping up again, lashing out with his hind legs, the air whistling as it does when one hits a really long drive with a golf club, and striking with his forefeet at the wooden walls.

I went in and spoke to him, and, for a moment, he was still; then he began again. He did not recognise me, or, indeed, know that I was there after the first moment. To escape his violence I jumped into the manger, and from there climbed on to a beam. Meantime a veterinary officer had been collected from an adjoining brigade of artillery. He clambered on to the beam with me and told me that he knew what was wrong. Warrior had swallowed a piece of sharp metal, shaped like a crooked nail, with his hay.

There had been several cases of it and most of the horses had died. Some thought the pieces of metal had been put in intentionally, but I should guess that it was an accident. At any rate the pain that they caused in the horses' intestines was agonising. The veterinary officer said that the best thing we could do was to let poor Warrior struggle to the utmost. It turned out that he was quite right, for the horrible piece of metal was in due course dislodged, and Warrior's life was saved. Within a week I was riding him about again, but I shall never forget that strange midnight scene in the battered stable. His faithful groom, Thomson, holding two lanterns, quite distraught with horror at the catastrophe which had befallen Warrior, the wild leaps of my poor horse, with trembling flesh, and wild red eye, the brave veterinary officer at last managing to calm him, and then the final collapse when we thought he was dead. In fact it was only a strong injection that eventually revived him.

I have lost sight of this veterinary officer who helped us on that night. If he has survived and reads this book, I hope he will write and tell me of his whereabouts, and come to the Isle of Wight to see the horse whose life he undoubtedly saved.

CHAPTER VIII

FROST AND SNOW ON THE SOMME

A cruel winter for horses—We are troubled by Richthofen's aeroplanes—Warrior rests by the sea—Christmas with his friends—Horseshows and gallops along the sands—Back to the Somme—Forward at last—The little battles of Equancourt and Guyencourt—Harvey's V.C.—Warrior wants to go on.

THE sombre close of the Battle of the Somme was cruel to horses no less than to men. The roads were so completely broken up by alternate frost, snow and rain, that the only way to get ammunition to the forward batteries was to carry it up in panniers slung on horses. Often these poor beasts, who were led forward in long strings with three shells on each side of them, would sink deep into the mud. Sometimes, in spite of all their struggles, they could not extricate themselves, and died where they fell.

Many times I accompanied these melancholy convoys with Warrior. He, too, would sometimes sink through the frozen crust into the oozing white mud below, but he was very strong, and when I jumped from his back he would somehow manage to get out, though he had one or two narrow escapes.

One of our troubles was that the famous airman, Richthofen, perhaps the bravest on either side of that most gallant band of flying men, well-nigh established

100

a local air supremacy for Germany. His observers would spot these convoys of horses, and direct their artillery fire on them, often with great effect; they would even swoop down and attack them with their machine guns. Of course our men were doing just the same thing to the Germans on the other side of the line.

It was a strange kind of warfare, and the Germans got rather the better of it so far as the horses were concerned. We found it necessary to move a great deal by day, but the Germans, somehow, contrived to make all their movements by night. I used often to fly over the lines during this period, and it was surprising to see the long convoys of horses and waggons on our side and not a thing moving behind the German trenches. Our horses suffered accordingly.

On one occasion when Warrior was stuck fast a German flew down and emptied his machine-gun belt at us; the bullets were very near, but not one of them hit us.

He had many other narrow escapes during this time. Once a great shell fell near him, and he was completely buried under the falling earth except for one forefoot. But with the help of a little digging we got him out unharmed, except for a lameness in the off-fore which has troubled him from time to time ever since.

In the cold grip of that bitter winter of 1916–17 the fighting on the Somme died down. Those of my men who had been acting as infantry went out of the line to rejoin their comrades with the horses. Warrior and I went with them.

I could see my dear horse, nearly worn out by the desperate experiences he had been through, reviving each day as he found himself with his old friends, men and horses alike. With us once again were my son Frank with his Arab pony, Akbar, with the queer little half-brown, half-white face, Antoine with his fine black horse, on whose back he was painted by Munnings a year later, and, above all, his great new friend, who had been my brigade major for many months, that famous horseman and horse lover, Geoffrey Brooke.

Of course these men had been with me more than half the time during our strenuous winter days on the Somme, but their horses had been back near the sea.

I have said that Warrior had an extraordinary gift of exciting the friendship and admiration of men. I shall never forget the cheers of the Canadians when I rode round the different regiments and batteries at Christmas time. They all shouted: "Warrior," ran up to him, asked him if he was all right, crowded round him, officers and men alike; he was, as always, very gracious, but a little aloof.

I rejoice to think that there are many Canadians still living, survivors of the desperate advances and retreats that were to follow, who remember those happy days of reunion at Christmas time, 1916.

But Warrior had some particular friends. They were all gathered together during this brief time of rest, all except Smith, my servant, who had been invalided home shortly before. There was Thomson, his groom, who accompanied him from the 8th of August, 1914, until Christmas Day, 1918, when he returned to England.

There was my son Frank, for whom he had a particular regard, partly because the boy had an extraordinary way with all creatures, horses especially, but dogs and birds too. Warrior was bound to him all the more by his affection for his Arab pony, Akbar.

Then there was Antoine, with his great black mare, of whom Warrior was frankly jealous because she was taller, and seemed grander than he was.

But, especially, there was his great new friend, Geoffrey Brooke. He had, and I have no doubt has still, the unique gift of making complete friends with any horse after only a few days of conversation. Looking back, I must confess that I was a little jealous of Geoffrey Brooke! Warrior recognised in him the supreme horseman, a title to which I can make no claim.

At intervals in the lull of battle we would have sports, including horse shows. Warrior and I used to put up some sort of a show when we happened to be out of the line, but when Geoffrey Brooke rode him, Warrior became the "star turn," and won every prize for good looks, for jumping, and for docility. He enjoyed it all; he rejoiced in being first in everything. With me he had only got second prizes, but with Geoffrey Brooke he was always first. Still, after the brief show was over, he would always come up to me

of his own accord, and rub his head against me,
explaining in his own language that for all ordinary
purposes he liked me best of all.

I wrote to Geoffrey Brooke in Egypt telling him of
this book, and asking him if he could write a word or
two about Warrior. This is what he sends me:

"You ask me if I remember Warrior, your old
veteran charger. Of course I do. Horses, like men, vary
in character, and he is one of the personalities that
one never forgets.

"An ideal charger of the short-legged thoroughbred type, never sick or sorry, never at a loss in an
emergency. I can picture him now at the head of the
Canadian Cavalry Brigade full of energy and life, yet
placid and as steady as a rock in the cataclysm of
battle. I think the last time I saw him was when we
met in Moreuil Wood. He always appeared to have
a spare leg when galloping over shell-torn ground,
and I know neither his master nor your staff for one
minute attached any blame to him when you broke
your leg one night in 'No Man's Land.' I can remember at least one occasion when I had the pleasure
of riding him with success in a horse show in France.

"Unselfish loyalty, indomitable courage, exhibit-
ing an entire disregard of danger, and a generous
nature, always giving of his best. These were the
qualities inherent in Warrior. What more does one
ask of a friend?

"I am delighted to hear that he is still going strong
and enjoying life. He deserves the best."

And so for a few brief weeks we were as happy together as we had been ten months before, re-forming our forces as a mounted brigade, getting men and horses fit. We were once again in the same billets, riding down to the same sea, and galloping along the same sands with the keen west wind blowing along the shores of Northern France. Warrior and I with Geoffrey Brooke on his bay gelding, Antoine and his upstanding black mare, Frank and his Akbar, and all the gay band of Canadian horsemen—Lord Strathcona's Horse, the Royal Canadians, the Royal Canadian Dragoons, the Fort Garry Horse, the Royal Canadian Horse Artillery. All of us had been through more than two years of strenuous warfare; we had lost half our number at least of men and horses. But all of us looked forward to continuing a struggle, against a gallant foe, which we were convinced we were bound to win.

As the horses got fitter and stronger we used to have great gallops along the sands together. From these gallops I learned that Akbar, the Arab, could go much the fastest for the first fifty yards, that Antoine's horse could head us all at a quarter of a mile, and Geoffrey Brooke's at half a mile. From that distance onwards it was always Warrior who was the leader. I used to reflect then that "Young Jim" had been right, and that had Warrior adopted a racing career he might have made himself famous in that field of activity.

Now that it is all over, or at any rate over for a time, I must confess that the genuine and deep

105

affection of my Canadian comrades in those three and a half strenuous years, was due, in the first degree, to my constant companion, Warrior.

With men and horses revived and fit, I daily expected orders either to go to Egypt or to try for a break through at Arras. The orders I received involved only my son Frank, who at his own request was to rejoin the Hampshire Regiment, to which he had been gazetted. This meant that he had to leave Akbar behind.

We had a last gallop together along the sands, Warrior and Akbar racing each other; then I drove him in a motor-car to rejoin his regiment. I got leave to spend a day or two with him and his distinguished regiment, and then returned to my command. He asked me to take care of Akbar, and I replied that Warrior would see to that. He was killed not long afterwards while leading his company.

On my return, I received secret orders to move back to the Somme battlefield. It was a long march, and we marched mostly by night. It was bitterly cold after sunset, with perpetual rain, sleet or snow; but the ground was drying up as it always does in early March in Northern France.

As we approached Amiens I received a message that the Germans were retiring from their position on the Somme battlefield, and we made a forced march by night to arrive at our named point at three o'clock in the morning. I had ridden Warrior all through this march except for a few hours when I changed to his inseparable friend, Akbar.

Now was Warrior's moment. Two and a half years before he had been through a dreadful retreat, chivvied about by the oncoming host, and clearly saying to me: "Why must we be always going away?" Then came a year and a half behind a rigid line with barrages and shells dropping behind and in front of him, and often those swift bullets which always worried him; never any advance.

If you live with a horse, as I did with Warrior all those years and have done since, you realise that he understands things in some ways even better than you do yourself. He hated this negative attitude. He was strong and fit and swift. Could he never go at the enemy, as all creatures long to do when they are attacked?

But the great moment for which he longed at last arrived. It was only a little battle when we captured Equancourt and Guyencourt on successive days, but, believe me, it was wonderful to feel this gallant horse between my legs thrilling to the moment when we galloped forward.

Some may remember that on the second day Harvey,* of Strathcona's, mounted on a Canadian horse, won the Victoria Cross which some think the most dramatic of the War. Warrior and I were galloping together in the neighbourhood when he achieved his marvellous feat of valour, and I can record that it was all I could do to prevent Warrior from joining in the desperate charge which Harvey led.

In those brief joyous moments of victory before the line was again "stabilised," to use that hateful phrase,

107

* Lieutenant Frederick Harvey earned the Victoria Cross for his conduct on 27 March 1917 in an attack on the village of Guyencourt. German soldiers defending the village opened fire with rifles and a machine gun at very close range on Harvey's leading troop as it advanced, causing heavy casualties. Lieutenant Harvey ran forward well ahead of his men, jumped the barbed wire protecting the enemy position, shot the machine gunner and captured the gun.

we advanced more miles in an hour than we had advanced yards in a month during the previous year. We had gained twenty miles from where we started.

After we had captured Guyencourt, I rode forward with Antoine and beheld a strange spectacle. A mile and a quarter to the eastward, in the sunlight of this bright winter's evening, I saw three squadrons of German cavalry drawn up facing us. Behind us my men were shepherding prisoners, and posting machine guns at various points in front of the little village and the small woods on the crest above it in order to repel the expected counter-attack. Our advance had been so swift that there was no artillery to support us; except for the crackling of ammunition dumps to which the enemy had set fire when they retired, there was, for the moment, complete silence.

How well I remember that moment, sitting astride my Warrior, rejoicing at having seen one of my men do a deed of valour that would live for ever, and looking over the flat plain before me at the strange spectacle of three squadrons of cavalry drawn up in battle array a mile and a half away.

Horses are gifted with marvellous sight; they can discern a single horse moving along a slope at four and five miles' distance. Warrior had seen the German horses; he neighed loudly, and tried to go forward.

I said to my A.D.C., Prince Antoine: "Warrior is right. Let's charge into the middle of them."

But Antoine was wiser than either Warrior or I. He knew it was no use contradicting me, but just said: "The horses are too tired to cover the distance at the gallop." So Warrior and I were restrained by a wise word.

Of course the enterprise would have been mad, and would have ended in utter disaster. These squadrons were paraded just outside the famous Hindenburg line at Epehey. Had we gone forward we should have been destroyed, for we had no means of turning a flank, and this story of Warrior would never have been written.

Nevertheless Warrior wanted to go on, though we had ridden far and fast that day.

CHAPTER IX

WITH THE TANKS AT CAMBRAI

Stuck in the mud—Warrior plays hide-and-seek with the shells at
Paschendaele—The horse in modern war—The tank attack at Cambrai
—Warrior meets Prince Rupprecht, but at a distance—Stopping the
gap—Vadencourt again—Warrior sits for his portrait.

FOR the next few weeks Warrior and I had quite a gay
time. I had built him quite a comfortable stable near
Vadencourt Château, a headquarters which the
Germans had recently evacuated.

Our sector of the new front line ran through the
outskirts of St. Quentin on both sides of the Omignon
River. Vadencourt was on the top of a ridge, then
there was a little valley, then another ridge before
the front line was reached. The question was how to
get to our front line in daylight, which I wanted to do
each day, without undue risk. The problem was
solved completely by galloping over the first ridge on
Warrior, and disappearing into the valley below.
The German gunners had not time to shoot at us as
we topped the ridge, and they could not possibly tell
which way we had turned when we went forward out
of view. But they would nearly always fire a salvo.
Of course the odds in our favour were far greater than
if we had been crossing Piccadilly in the traffic, and
this Warrior thoroughly appreciated. I could almost

110

hear him laugh as the shells dropped hundreds of yards away, and I know he enjoyed the adventure.

Although we did not then know it, this was the place which had already been chosen for the greatest attack, so far as numbers were concerned, in the whole history of war. As a consequence the Germans wanted to keep the place fairly quiet. This was very convenient for Warrior, because, except on one occasion, no shells fell near his stable, and he could sleep in comfort.

This gay time, for even war can be gay, was brought to an abrupt end by my being knocked out during a successful little attack that we made. In addition to surface wounds, I had seven small bones broken in the one crash; I just survived, and was invalided home, while Warrior stayed behind. But within seven weeks we were together again in France, just in time to join in the ill-fated battle of Paschendaele.

During that winter of 1917 Warrior had some very hard times, exhausting times, cruel times; the march to the Battle of Paschendaele was one of them.

Once again the strange idea prevailed that the Germans were so exhausted that they could not fight much longer, and that we of the cavalry could gallop through, and turn the retreat into a rout.

So we loaded ourselves up with provisions and hand grenades, and great quantities of ammunition for our machine-gunners. And thus encumbered we marched north to Ypres.

I have said that Warrior never flinched from a shell after the first few days. Except for a steam-roller he would shy at nothing, but as we approached Ypres he shied so violently that I very nearly fell off. What had so disturbed him was a party of some hundreds of Chinamen digging graves. I found it difficult to get him to go on, and he trembled all over. What was in dear Warrior's mind so to alarm his imperturbable soul I shall never know.

Heavy rains had already begun to fall, and our camp a little way west of Ypres was deep in mud. Again my brigade was to have the honour of leading the "break through." So I thought I had better go to look at the place indicated, the remnant of the village of Paschendaele.

Warrior went with me through the ruins of Ypres, as he had often done before, with Sir John French on his back three years earlier during the First Battle of Ypres. Past the remnants of the Cloth Hall and the cathedral we went together, and so out to St. Julien.

The north-west wind, and the pitiless rain beat down upon us in a way I shall never forget as we rode through St. Julien, and thence along a corduroy road. After a time even the road seemed to disappear. There were many dead horses lying about which had foundered in the mud, and could not be extricated. All of a sudden Warrior went deep into the mud up to his belly. Antoine was just behind me with Corporal King and another orderly. It was only with immense difficulty that the four of us managed to get him back on to sounder ground, but it was a narrow escape.

So we sent the horses back, and Antoine and I went forward on foot. It took us three hours to do less than

THE FORT GARRY'S ON THE MARCH;
ONE OF MUNNINGS'S FIRST PICTURES,
DRAWN ON THE OMIGNON FRONT IN
THE WINTER OF 1917–18.

113

as many miles to the front line, where we saw very clearly that the mud was so deep that even if all the Germans went away, infantry could hardly move, and cavalry not at all.

The horses suffered terribly at the Battle of Paschendaele, even more than in the Battle of the Somme a year before. But I would like to record that one of the finest things about that indomitable creature, the English soldier of the front line, was his invariable kindness and, indeed, his gentleness at all times to the horses. I hardly ever saw a man strike a horse in anger during all the four years of war, and again and again I have seen a man risk his life, and, indeed, lose it, for the sake of his horse. This applies in equal degree to the cavalry, the artillery, engineers, transport, in fact, every branch of our army.

Between 1914 and 1918 hundreds of thousands of horses were employed on the Western Front, as they must be in every war. People who do not understand the realities of warfare think that horses are not required on modern battlefields. They think that all battles will be conducted by mechanical means. So they will be for the first few days, then it will be the horse. Truly the horse might cry out more loudly than any other creature, "Give peace in our time, O Lord."

The fighting at Paschendaele came to its melancholy close, and Warrior and I trekked south from Ypres with the Canadian Cavalry Brigade.

The wet and the mud had told upon Warrior's health. Even his indomitable spirit began to grow weary and he had lost some of his spring, though he stuck it out gallantly during the long marches which followed.

Not long after I was told, as a great secret, of the proposed mass tank attack on Cambrai. Yet again, they told me, my brigade was to have the honour of leading the advance. The secret was so well kept that even the Cabinet at home did not know of the impending attack, and when it happened on 20th November, it came as a complete surprise, not only to His Majesty's Ministers, but to the Germans in that sector.

For a few hours it was a glorious success. It was fine to be cantering along just behind a tank into the village of Masnières. I am sure Warrior enjoyed every minute of it. Down the main street of Masnières we went together, Warrior's nose nearly touching the tank as it reached the bridge over the Canal de l'Escaut. Then misfortune befell the adventure, for with a frightful bang the bridge collapsed, and the tank fell through into the canal! Warrior and I very nearly fell in too, but we just avoided it. There was a good deal of rifle-fire going on, and many of the horses behind us were hit, but Warrior's luck held, and although he was the leading horse, he escaped without a scratch.

We managed to build some sort of a narrow bridge a little to the south of the one that had been demolished, and one of my squadrons got over. The leader of it, Strachan, of Fort Garry's Horse, received the Victoria Cross for making a mounted charge on the German batteries, but, of course, the idea of the great "break through" had come to an end, for darkness was falling and it would have taken us a very long time to get the whole brigade over the two planks of which our bridge consisted. Added to this, the cavalry to our left had been completely held up.

During the next three days, we stayed at Masnières and from time to time made a few little attacks on foot; the bridging of the canal for artillery and cavalry was impossible owing to close-range rifle-fire. I rode Warrior on a reconnaissance up towards Crévecœur Spur, which the Germans still held. He had another lucky escape that morning, for many of the horses who were with me were shot at fairly close range.

Some years afterwards I saw Prince Rupprecht of Bavaria, who was commanding the army opposed to us. From him I learned that he also was on Crévecœur Spur that morning. From the map he showed me, I estimated that Warrior cannot have been within more than six hundred yards of that redoubtable army commander. Prince Rupprecht remembered the episode and the galloping horsemen. Some day I hope he will come here and renew acquaintance with my old horse.

But by the fourth day we were withdrawn, leaving the infantry in the dangerous salient caused by the successful tank attack. I received orders to take my brigade into a back area for a real rest and refit, which we sorely needed, but we halted for a time about six miles behind the line.

It has been my experience in two wars that whenever you are told you are going for a long rest you are always needed almost at once for some desperate enterprise. So it was in this case.

On the very morning that we were starting on our long march towards the sea, I was wakened at daybreak by Geoffrey Brooke with the news that there had been a disaster of the first magnitude, and that we were needed to stem the onrush of the victorious Germans.

Within twenty minutes I was on Warrior's back galloping to meet General MacAndrew, who commanded our division. He told me that we had lost all the ground we had gained ten days before, that about eight thousand men had been made prisoners in addition to many casualties, and that eighty guns had also been captured with many hundreds of machine guns.

Here was a disaster of the first order, or so we thought at the time, not foreseeing the wrath to come on the 21st March in the following year.

The Germans were about a mile and a half from where we stood talking. I remember the words I used—a conversation I have recalled in my book *Adventure*—"I suppose you would like us to blow into the battle, and see what we can do," and his reply: "That's about the size of it."

So, with my signal troop, Warrior and I went forward to have a look. There was a row of trees which screened us from the ridge where I knew the Germans to be, so there was no shell-fire to bother us, and we were in comparative security. From the rifle-fire I heard I guessed, and I proved to be right, that this ridge was for the moment only lightly held.

The brigade came on and joined me in a fold of the ground, and I told the colonels of my plan. They would endeavour to gallop the ridge, and then extend to right and left. The Royal Canadian Dragoons were the leading regiment, so they were chosen for the attack.

On all such occasions as these when the decision was taken to advance, Warrior became a changed horse. He would quiver between my knees, not at all from fear, but from the joy of battle, and when we started to gallop, as had happened at Equancourt, then at Guyencourt, at the First Battle of Cambrai ten days before, and again now, I could feel the great muscles of his body extending as he bounded forward.

Through my telescope I had seen that a thin strand of wire ran through the trees, but I reckoned that it would easily be broken. The leading squadron of Dragoons galloped right through it, and on to the ridge. The Germans were taken so completely by surprise that very few of my men were hit. We captured several of the enemy, and occupied their improvised trench. Then we pressed forward, spreading out as we went. But at last we were held up, and consolidated our position as best we could. I had ridden Warrior all that day, and although there was much rifle-fire and shelling, he escaped unscathed.

We found him a comfortable place for the night in an old deep trench with a piece of corrugated iron for a roof.

Next day the Germans pressed forward on both sides of us. Strathcona's made an attack and captured several hundreds of the enemy, together with twenty machine guns and quantities of ammunition. So we became almost impregnable.

It was embarrassing to be so nearly surrounded, but it had a great merit in that we were almost immune from shell-fire; the Germans could not send over high explosives at us without the danger of hitting their own men too.

After two days and a half in this extraordinary position a brigade of the Guards and the Indian cavalry came up and our position was saved. The Indian cavalry made a desperate charge, and, although they lost a great number of men and horses, managed to seize a little wood which enfiladed us, and had been the cause of a great many of our casualties. We were greatly reduced in numbers ourselves, and I was glad when the infantry took over the position on the evening of the third day.

Here another bit of luck befell Warrior. I had another horse with me, which I had named St. Quentin. I got on his back to ride round and supervise the relief. When it was nearly complete a bullet struck poor St. Quentin in the neck, and he fell stone dead. Incidentally he fell on me, to my great advantage, for the smash, though painful, broke down all the adhesions in my left arm which, for the last four months, had prevented me lifting my left hand higher than my neck.

I don't know why I chose St. Quentin instead of Warrior that day, but it so happened.

At last we returned to a quiet place for rest, refit and reinforcement. But after a week or two Warrior and I were back in the line again, just before Christmas, taking over our old familiar section of the front near the Omignon River. This time my headquarters were at a place we called Small Foot Wood, about a mile north of Vadencourt, where they had been eight months before. Warrior had quite a nice hut to live in.

It was in this part of the world that Warrior first made friends with a very remarkable person, no less than the man who, with characteristic generosity, illustrates this book: A. J. Munnings, R.A.

He was not then as famous as he is now, but even then discerning folk saw in him the most brilliant painter of horses of his day, and perhaps of all time.

He turned up one morning in plain clothes, in this bleak area, where for months no human being had been seen in anything but French, English or German uniform. Of course it had never been the intention of the Canadian authorities that Munnings should join us in the front line, but this whimsical and gallant soul thought that this was just the best place in which to be. And so it turned out, for by common consent his paintings and drawings of the Canadian horses, close up against the front line, are some of the most brilliant things he has ever done.

THIS IS THE PORTRAIT OF WARRIOR,
NOW IN CANADA, WHICH MUNNINGS
PAINTED IN FRANCE. WARRIOR AND I
HAD JUST RETURNED FROM OUR
OWN FRONT LINE. THE GERMAN
FRONT LINE IS IN THE BACKGROUND,
A FEW THOUSAND YARDS AWAY.

121

As I rode back from the front line one cold morning, covered with mud, I met this strange apparition in civilian clothes. Munnings said: "Come along, I want to paint you." So Warrior and I had to stand stock still while the eminent man drew us.

It was a bitterly cold day and painting a portrait in the open air must have been both difficult and unpleasant. The frost of the night before had left a thin crust on the top of the ground, and through this the unfortunate Munnings kept breaking into the mud underneath until I had him mounted on some duckboards. Moreover, I could only spare him little more than an hour and kept producing my watch and telling him how many minutes he had left. However, he reminds me that when we adjourned for lunch I took pity on him and ordered out one of the remaining bottles of my best claret.

The portrait was finished in the afternoon with my orderly taking my place on Warrior, adorned in one of my spare caps and tunics. This unusual experience had its embarrassing side for him, as several officers of my staff saluted him in passing in mistake for me and he did not know whether to go through with the impersonation and acknowledge their salutes or pretend not to notice them!

The portrait is now in Canada, but a drawing of it is reproduced here. The background, at a distance of about three thousand five hundred yards, was German territory. Probably that fact would have deterred most artists from choosing such a place in which to paint a portrait. Not so Munnings; he seemed to think that it added greatly to its interest. Warrior was not of the same opinion, and showed his displeasure by pawing and snorting. However, he made it up with Munnings, who was later on destined to be with him, and actually to ride him, during his greatest ordeal— the Retreat of March 1918, which we call the Battle of Amiens.

CHAPTER X

WARRIOR'S GREAT ADVENTURE

The retreat of March 1918—More narrow escapes—The falling
house—A critical moment of the War—Warrior leads the charge on
Moreuil Wood—-The German version—Marshal Foch's tribute.

ON the 18th March, 1918, I handed over my command at Vadencourt to the infantry, and rode away
on Warrior from Small Foot Wood. But again, as at
Cambrai, hopes of a long rest were doomed to
disappointment.

Munnings was with me, and we rode to the château
of the Marquis de Bargemont, where Warrior was
housed in a magnificent stable. He had never seen
anything like it since he had left Freddie Guest's
stable at Burley-on-the-Hill.

Here my friend Orpen turned up from Amiens, and
painted a picture of me, while Munnings painted one of
my beloved aide-de-camp, Prince Antoine of Orleans,
on his black horse. He had planned to make another
picture of Warrior. Then the great attack fell, and
again we blew into the battle. This time the disaster
was indeed of the first magnitude.

Ludendorff, in his memoirs, says that the Germans
captured eighty thousand unwounded prisoners on
this occasion, but our men fought hard enough, as
the frightful German casualties showed. I have been

told they lost a quarter of a million killed and wounded in the first ten days of the fighting, but, nevertheless, with desperate courage they still advanced.

We fought many little rearguard actions, at one time covering the French Corps commanded by General Diebold. I well remember one of these days, I think on the 26th March, sitting on Warrior on a little bridge over a stream, giving orders to Colonel Macdonald, commanding Strathcona's Horse. A single shot rang out, fired from the rushes quite near to us, and Macdonald's horse fell dead. His horse's nose and Warrior's were almost touching, but it is wonderful to be able to record that Warrior did not flinch although he knew full well the dangers of rifle-fire.

I had Akbar and Patrick with me as well as Warrior, and had acquired another horse to take the place of St. Quentin, who had been killed at the Second Battle of Cambrai. So I rode Warrior on about every third day during this period.

On the morning of the 27th March Warrior had a most extraordinary escape. I have recounted the story in my book *Adventure*, but it will bear telling again.

I had stabled Warrior the night before in the drawing-room of a little French villa which was still completely intact—so much so that I remember giving him his corn on a small ormolu table.

At dawn the next morning I stood in the square of the little village dictating orders to my brigade major. The Germans, who were not far off, perceived that the village was occupied, and opened fire with a big naval gun. Almost the first shell that came over our heads hit the little villa fair and square and exploded inside, knocking it completely down except for one corner.

I said to Connolly: "I am afraid that is the end of Warrior." But, no, there was his head poking out from the few bricks still standing, with the joist of the ceiling resting on his back.

We started to try to pull the bricks away, but before we had got very far with it, Warrior made a supreme effort and bounded out. As he emerged the joist fell, and the whole of the remaining corner of the house collapsed in a heap.

Except for a little lameness from having carried most of the weight of the top storey, Warrior was none the worse, and I rode him all that day.

On the night of the 29th March we camped at a little village called Boves near the main line from Paris to Amiens. Things looked very black then. I knew that if the Germans reached the ridge covering Amiens, the French and English armies had orders to fall back, the French on Paris, the English on the Channel Ports.

Next morning early, General Pitman, who commanded our division, woke me where I was sleeping close to Warrior under a wall. He told me that the German advance had continued, that they had captured the vital Moreuil Ridge, but that our infantry were holding on, much reduced in numbers, to the left of Moreuil village, which was for the moment held by the French. He directed me to take my brigade in that direction in order to help the infantry, and to

THE CANADIAN CAVALRY WATERING.
A STUDY PAINTED BY MUNNINGS
DURING THE LONG MARCH PRE-
CEDING THE ATTACK ON THE
MOREUIL RIDGE.

cover their retirement when it became necessary. His last words were: "Don't get too heavily involved; you will be badly needed later."

Again, as at the Second Battle of Cambrai, I jumped on Warrior and galloped forward with my brigade major, Connolly (who had succeeded Geoffrey Brooke, promoted to command the 16th Lancers), my aide-de-camp, Prince Antoine, and my signal troop.

Although he must have been weary, Warrior put up a good gallop, and we clattered into the little village of Castel in fine style. There were a good many bullets flying down the road, but by turning to the right behind some houses we were in complete security.

By great good fortune I found the French divisional commander there. It seemed to me quite clear that unless we re-captured the Moreuil Ridge it was all over with Amiens, and probably with the Allied cause. I told the Frenchman this, and he agreed with me, but added that my little brigade could not possibly achieve it. In this he was wrong, as the event proved, but the main thing was that he sent orders to his men to hold on to the village of Moreuil on our right.

Sitting there on Warrior's back I decided to attempt the apparently impossible—to recapture the Moreuil Ridge.

Warrior was strangely excited, all trace of exhaustion had gone; he pawed the ground with impatience. In some strange way, without the least doubt, he knew that the crisis in his life had come.

At this moment the colonels of each of my regiments came galloping up as we had arranged. I dismounted and gave Warrior to Corporal King to hold. We consulted briefly, and orders were written for the attack. Then they galloped back to rejoin their regiments, the leading one, the Royal Canadian Dragoons, being only half a mile away.

The plan was that I should cross the little river separating Castel from the Bois de Moreuil with my staff and my signal troop, and, as the brigade advanced, should go forward with the signal troop and plant my little triangular red flag at the point of the wood. Our infantry were only some four hundred yards from this point, and were firing into the wood. It seemed clear to me that under cover of their fire I could do this vital thing, and establish the flag and headquarters at the point of the wood so that every man could see, as he passed our infantry front line, that the first phase of the battle had been won.

Now comes the wonderful part of the story as it concerns Warrior. As I have said elsewhere, after nearly four years of war Warrior had learnt to disregard shell-fire, as being part of ordinary war risks, but he had learnt to show great respect for rifle-fire, and would always try to swerve to right or left in order, as he clearly understood, to reduce the danger from it. But this day all was changed.

I bade farewell to my French comrade, and mounted Warrior. As I rode round the corner of the little house behind which we had been consulting into the main road of Castel, Warrior took charge and galloped as hard as he could straight for the front line. At the bottom of the hill, where we were in dead ground, I induced him to slow down to a trot as we crossed the stream by a little half-broken bridge. Then up the opposing slant we went, still out of direct view of the enemy, and across a field of winter wheat. A hundred yards beyond us was our own thin front line of infantry, lying down and returning the enemy fire.

There were about twenty of us all told when I halted Warrior for a moment and looked round to give final orders. I turned in my saddle and told my comrades that the faster we galloped the more certain we were of success, that I would tell the infantry to redouble their fire as we passed through them, and that the day was as good as ours. But I could hardly finish my sentence before Warrior again took charge.

He was determined to go forward, and with a great leap started off. All sensation of fear had vanished from him as he galloped on at racing speed. He bounded into the air as we passed our infantry, and I remember shouting to a young infantry officer just on my left: "Fire as fast as you can."

There was, of course, a hail of bullets from the enemy as we crossed the intervening space and mounted the hill, and perhaps half of us were hit, but Warrior cared for nothing. His one idea was to get at the enemy. He almost buried his head in the brushwood when we reached the point of the wood at the chosen spot. We were greeted by twenty or thirty Germans, who fired a few shots before running, doubtless thinking there were thousands of us following.

Corporal King jammed his lance with the red flag into the ground, the survivors of my signal troop jumped off their horses and ran into the wood with their rifles, and the first phase of the battle was over. It was perhaps an odd way to use a signal troop, but it was the only thing to do.

But what I must record, and it is indeed the truth, is that so far as I am concerned the credit for this wild adventure, which succeeded in so miraculous a fashion, was due not to me, but to my horse Warrior. He it was who did not hesitate, and did not flinch, though well he knew the danger from those swift bullets which he had seen kill so many hundreds of men and horses all around him in the preceding years.

It was a wonderful day. The main attack swept up and the wood was soon filled with galloping Canadian horsemen. Both sides, ours and the Germans', seemed to be filled with some extraordinary exaltation. Neither would surrender. Again and again these brave Bavarians and Saxons too, and men from every part of Germany, surrounded and wounded, would continue to fire, but, on either side, not one man would hold up his hands and surrender. One determined Bavarian, with a sword thrust right through his neck, raised his rifle just level with Warrior's near shoulder, and had a last shot before he died.

Freiherr von Falkenstein, a captain commanding a company of the 2nd Battalion of the 101st Grenadiers (one of the regiments opposed to us), wrote an account of it which has recently seen the light.

"The Canadians were able to charge right home into the front line of the infantry, where a very desperate hand-to-hand fight ensued, the horsemen engaging the Grenadiers at first with their pistols, and then, when these were discharged, taking to their swords and falling upon the Saxons, cutting and thrusting, the infantry offering a stubborn opposition. And for some moments the battle raged to and fro, and in and out of the wood, among fallen men and horses. . . . A small scattered party of Strathcona's came suddenly upon the rear of No. 7 Company and endeavoured—taken aback and dismounted as many of them were—to cut their way through. Very few, however, succeeded in doing so; not one of them allowed himself to be taken prisoner—each man had kept the last round in his pistol for himself!"

Such was the spirit of the men who took part in this desperate action. So it was with the horses, and especially with Warrior, who, as all my surviving Canadian comrades will testify, was an outstanding example to all on that fateful day.

Another tribute to the heroism of the Canadian Cavalry Brigade was that paid by Marshal Foch himself, Commander-in-Chief of the French and British armies on that day. Here are his words: "On the 30th March the Battle was at the gates of Amiens, and at all hazards it was necessary to maintain the union of the armies. The Canadian Cavalry by their magnificent attack first held the enemy in check, and then definitely broke their forward march. In great degree, thanks to them, the situation, which was agonising at the beginning of the battle, was restored."

I never look at Warrior without remembering that he had a part, and so far as I was concerned, the main part, in achieving that success.

CHAPTER XI

THE FINAL ADVANCE

Warrior falls lame—And so escapes from death—A sixty-mile march—Warrior outlasts his master—Who returns to England—The final advance.

THE morning after the great day of 30th March, I mounted Warrior, tired but fit and well, and rode round the regiments of the brigade, and read to them the messages I had received from Haig, Commander-in-Chief, and Rawlinson, now commanding the Army.

We were lying in a wood, called the Bois de Senekat, two or three miles west of the Moreuil Ridge, which we had re-captured at so great a sacrifice of men and horses.

When Warrior and I got to our headquarters in the wood I remember giving him his corn, and then lying flat on the ground to rest while I saw him eat it. Then I fell asleep. I was wakened by one of Pitman's staff, who told me that we were to attempt next morning the recapture of the Hangard Ridge, and that there was to be a conference that evening as soon as all could be summoned.

A little dazed, and very tired, I mounted Warrior and rode to the place indicated. It was a ten-mile ride, and some of it was on a hard road covered with sharp flints. As we approached the rendezvous, Warrior trod on one of these flints with his off-fore when trotting at a good pace in the darkness. His feet went sliding in all directions and he nearly fell. When he had pulled himself together and stood up again he was hopelessly lame. Ever since that day his off-fore has been apt to give him trouble, for in addition to the injury to his foot, he badly twisted his fetlock and knee joint.

At the conference, it was unanimously decided that I should be in charge of the attack. Pitman wrote me a letter a little while ago saying that the reason for this decision was for no merit of my own except that I was the only man who could keep awake at the time!

However, so it was settled. I got Warrior back to my headquarters in the wood with great difficulty, but it was obviously hopeless to attempt to ride him next day. Akbar was lame, too, but there remained the black horse I had got in place of St. Quentin. So it was with him that I rode a few hours later to the point of assembly. My staff captain had arranged for a spare horse to be led as well. It was a time and place where motor-cars could not function at all. Everything had to be done on horseback, or on foot. So it was as well to have a spare horse.

The attack on the Hangard Ridge was a complete success, thanks to the extraordinary skill and gallantry of the cavalry regiments, home and dominion, who took part in it. But during the day my black horse was killed, and incidentally I swallowed a good deal of gas myself—one escape for Warrior.

I got on to the spare horse, and again rode round the captured position. Meantime the faithful staff captain had somehow borrowed another spare horse, and put him in a little ruined courtyard at the east end of the village of Hangard. There I returned towards evening and handed over my second horse to Corporal King. Having sent many messages by mounted orderlies, I proposed to ride round again, and was on the point of starting when a shell dropped in the courtyard, and both my horses were killed. Corporal King's horse was killed, too, though he miraculously survived. It was not until two o'clock in the morning that that day came to an end, after I had handed over the captured position to the infantry. It was on a mule led by the faithful Corporal King that I made most of my way back to headquarters! Had not Warrior trodden on that stone the evening before, he must quite certainly have been killed that day.

By the beginning of April, Warrior was stabled on the eastern outskirts of Amiens. There was still much shelling, but the violence of the attack gradually died down. So we had time to look after Warrior's bad leg, and in a couple of days he could put his weight on it again. Then we moved up to Albert, which every one of those who were there will remember, because of the figure of the Virgin on top of the church tower, hanging upside down.

We were quartered just west of the high ground covering Albert, which for the moment was occupied by the Germans, but here, too, the enemy could advance no farther, and Warrior's leg had time to

CANADIAN HORSES IN SHELTERS
CAMOUFLAGED AGAINST AIR OBSER-
VATION. WARRIOR IS IN THIS
PICTURE, WHICH WAS DRAWN BY
MUNNINGS A DAY OR TWO BEFORE
THE GREAT GERMAN ATTACK OF
MARCH 1918.

recover entirely. I was grateful for these few days of rest, for it was not long before there came a further ordeal for my gallant horse. A portion of the front line north of Béthune, mostly held by Portuguese troops, was completely caved in by a skilfully devised attack conducted by Prince Rupprecht in person, to the accompaniment of an exceptionally violent artillery barrage. I received orders to move north at all speed with the whole of my command, including a considerable force of machine guns which had been added to me.

It was clear that the Ypres Salient was again menaced, and, indeed, that the whole garrison might be cut off. The Channel Ports would then have been at the mercy of the enemy. So we were urged to move forward with all speed.

Dear Warrior did not fail on this long march. I rode him for sixty miles. I know he would have liked to lie down and rest, almost to lie down and die, after the first twenty miles, but he stuck it out. All honour to him. We did help again to stem the tide of battle, and, without doubt, old Warrior played his part.

In time the great onslaught in the Valley of the Lys, which involved the capture of Bailleuil, and for a time of Mont Kemel, died down and we rode back by easier stages to the neighbourhood of Albert. The quantity of gas which I had swallowed at Hangard Ridge had reduced me to a man who could do nothing much but cough, and I was taken back to the base hospital. The clever people there did wonders for me, and revived me once more. They wanted to send me straight home, but I managed to get back to my command, and to Warrior. But it was no good, and to my infinite chagrin a day came when I was ordered to report at the War Office the next morning.

I left Warrior in charge of Colonel Patterson, my second-in-command, telling him that I should soon be back again. But, of course, when I got to the War Office, although they all tried to be kind to me and promised me an early return, I could see that the doctors had determined to keep me away from France for some months.

I remember meeting Lord Milner, who was then Secretary of State for War, and telling him that except for a slight cough I was perfectly well, that I had left my horse in France, from whom I had never been separated all through the War, and could he not send me back? He promised that he would do so, and said that he would appoint me to what he called a suitable command, so I wrote to Patterson asking him to take care of Warrior until my return.

But for the succeeding months I did not return except for one or two brief visits on duty. Still with the promise of an early return to the Western Front, I was appointed Vice-Chairman of the Munitions Council, or as one of my friends phrased it, "Chief of Frightfulness." One thing I learned during that strange period, when all the greatest scientists in England were there to help, was that the horse is the most vital element in modern war. I do not say that all these great scientists will agree with me, though I know that some of them do, but I commend this conclusion to those who may read this book, in the hope that while praying for peace they may make sure of an adequate supply of horses in time of war.

General Patterson, for he was soon promoted to command the Canadian Mounted Brigade in my stead, took the greatest care of Warrior. Indeed, I know that for this short period he tried to keep him out of the greater risks, and I shall always be grateful to him for doing so. But I have not the least doubt that Warrior was thoroughly displeased!

In every letter I received from my Canadian friends of all ranks they made reference to him. He had become a legend amongst these gallant men, as, indeed, he is to this day.

Then the Germans retired, encompassed by a host of foes, their women and children starving behind them, and their Rhineland towns subjected to incessant bombardments by Trenchard's independent air force. It was perhaps the most remarkable, sustained and courageous enterprise in the history of this extraordinary war. After four years with nearly the whole world leagued against them, these brave Germans retired at last.

I found General Patterson and my beloved Warrior at Valenciennes. Everyone was very hungry, including Warrior. He was frankly overjoyed to see me, but I think a little disappointed that I could give him nothing except one biscuit, which he ate voraciously. Ever since that day, I think it was the 1st of November,

1918, I have tried to make up for my sad failure to get Warrior enough to eat.

Then came the Armistice, and kind General Patterson contrived to send Warrior, still accompanied by the faithful Thomson, back to the Isle of Wight in time for Christmas. There were many there who rejoiced to see him come home.

CHAPTER XII

PEACE

Meeting the Canadians in Hyde Park—and "Casey"—Victory marches—Point-to-Points—Fox-hunting—Warrior goes lame—But is restored to health—His long memory—Takes the Salute—In the limelight at Olympia—His life at Mottistone.

WHEN the War ended I was made Vice-President of the Air Council, and especially charged with the duty of demobilising the greater part of our wonderful Air Force, which, by that time, had become far and away the most powerful in the world. But I had also to help in sending home my faithful Canadian comrades with whom I had served for three and a half years on the Western Front. When they returned to England on their way to Canada, I took Warrior with me to see them in their camp in eastern Hampshire.

Then Warrior found himself involved in victory marches. By this time he was quite recovered from all the shocks of war, and enjoyed life supremely. How well I remember galloping along the grass in Hyde Park to the place where my Canadian cavalrymen were waiting! A shout went up: "Here's old Warrior!" The men crowded round him to pat him, and make much of him. He knew many of them. He could greet some horses, too, who had survived

PEACE

the War with him, and most famous of them all, Casey, General Archie Macdonnell's famous horse, who, like himself, had served most of the four years and escaped alive.

Warrior had first met Casey at Maresfield Park in January 1915. His master, perhaps I had better say his friend, Colonel Archie Macdonnell, was then commanding the Royal Canadians, Lord Strathcona's Horse, formed largely from the North-West Mounted Police. Casey could do all sorts of tricks, which Warrior had not learned, such as lying down and pretending to be dead, and then jumping suddenly up when Archie Macdonnell whispered in his ear, "The Kaiser." All this had intrigued Warrior very much, and he had tried to imitate the tricks. They were together for a year of the War. Then Archie Macdonnell became a divisional commander, and they lost sight of one another. There was ever such a whinnying and snorting when Warrior and Casey met in Hyde Park that day.

And so to the Victory March. I had a feeling as I rode on Warrior through the streets of London that my wise horse was rather bored by the whole business.

At one moment, Mr. John Burns, who had been my colleague in the Cabinet before the War, jumped out into the middle of the road with a kindly greeting to me, saying: "I am glad that you have brought the old horse back." He will remember how Warrior cast a curious eye upon him at this unexpected intervention in the proceedings, and that he rubbed his head violently against his shoulder.

143

However, the celebrations died down, as the battles had done before, and Warrior returned to the Isle of Wight.

How he rejoiced to be home again, to ride into the sea once more with me or one of my children, to stride up to the big downs and there to gallop over the soft turf! He was indeed a terrible handful at these times. My second daughter, Irene, loved to ride him, but he gave her some bad frights by starting off at the great speed which the English thoroughbred can attain, leaving his faithful little friend, Akbar, toiling a hundred yards behind in the first three hundred covered.

But Warrior was always kind to me, and, even out hunting, would never attempt to take hold unless I hurt his mouth by accident.

It was at this time that "Young Jim" suggested to me that although Warrior had been through such a desperate time at the War, being buried, battered and bashed in all manner of adventures, nevertheless he was still the fastest horse in the island. Had not his father Straybit won the Isle of Wight Point-to-Point just before the War? Was not his mother Cinderella of the race that breeds the fastest horses? Would it not be a romantic thing, if, after more than four years of war, much of it in the front line, Cinderella's son should win the race that his father had won fifteen years before?

I could only agree, and we started to train him on Mottistone Down.

Warrior enjoyed this training more than any horse

I have ever seen or known. He entered thoroughly into the spirit of the thing, and enjoyed himself enormously, whether it were the hours of walking exercise, the quiet canter, the occasional fast burst of speed, or the full mile gallop. He was all ready for the race in March 1921.

I wanted "Young Jim" to ride him, but he said that my nephew, Jim Seely, who, though young, was a very fine horseman, should be his jockey. And so it was arranged.

Now for years, indeed ever since I had first ridden Warrior on "Sidling Paul" three years before the War, I had had a private arrangement with him. It is not often that you want your horse to go at his best speed, and it is a good plan to have a private signal to tell him about it when you do. I had arranged with Warrior to bend forward close to his right ear, and make a little sibilant noise. This was the signal for the great effort of extreme speed. It was only rarely that I dared to use it because Warrior loved the joke of the thing, and would set off so fast that it was a very long business to pull him up again.

I told my nephew this, but in the course of the race he forgot all about it. When the horses were within three hundred yards from the winning-post we saw that Warrior was about two hundred yards behind the leading three. Obviously, the race was over, with Warrior last. Then Jim remembered. He bent forward and gave the signal. Those who saw the race will remember the extraordinary sight as Warrior suddenly seemed to spring to life and gallop at least

WARRIOR TAKING ME FOR A HUNT WITH THE
ISLE OF WIGHT FOX-HOUNDS AFTER THE WAR.

three yards to the other horses' one. But, alas! he was not quite in time and was beaten by a length.

I went to see him at once. He was snorting with rage. I have never seen my dear old horse so angry. He understood the whole business perfectly. He was prepared to bite or kick anybody!

My nephew was destined to win a great many other point-to-points in far more arduous circumstances, but he was equally distressed with Warrior that day.

But it all came right in the end, as things always do, for the next year nephew Jim insisted that "Young Jim" should be the jockey.

The same preparations were made and Warrior had completely recovered from his disappointment of the year before.

The great day came; it was the 30th March, 1922, and Warrior sailed home to victory, ridden by "Young Jim," who had first brought him into the world, on the anniversary of that great day when he had galloped through the British and German front lines to save Amiens and the Allied Cause.

It was a glorious day. Everyone was pleased. I could not bear to have him led away, and we rode home together over the downs rejoicing in this splendid conclusion of an anniversary which neither of us could ever forget.

Both before and after Warrior won the point-to-point he had quite a gay time each winter, for not only did I go fox-hunting with him whenever I had the time, but he became the family hunter.

My son Patrick hunted him constantly, and often

found himself near the head of the hunt, partly because he wished to be there, and partly because Warrior would not allow it to be otherwise. One mishap they had together which nearly ended in disaster.

There was a sheep-net fence running across a grass field with a gap hurdle at the north end of it. Hounds were running very fast; Patrick and Warrior were well ahead. Patrick rode at the hurdle, but Warrior for once did not see the wire; he swerved a little, got his knees in the wire at twenty-five miles an hour or more, and turned over like a shot rabbit. Both horse and rider were completely knocked-out by the violence of the blow. Warrior had his off-fore clean through the wire netting; the man who saw the smash said the wonder was his leg was not wrenched right off. It so happened that it was the same leg which had been crushed when he was buried under the fallen house at the end of March 1918, and we thought he would be lame for months afterwards; in fact, he was none the worse after a day or two. On the other hand, Patrick broke his collar bone very badly. But in a few weeks that was mended too, so Patrick and Warrior continued the chase together whenever I was not available.

In the summer time, my daughters would ride him, but out hunting he was too much for them. Even to-day, at twenty-six years of age, he is nearly too much for me, whom he knows so well, when hounds run fast, and another horse passes him.

About four years ago one of our rare disagreements

149

took place; it was entirely my own fault, as it generally has been. In the middle of a good hunt, when hounds were near their fox, we came to a fence which looked so high as to be nearly unjumpable, and with an awkward downhill landing. The best place to take it seemed to be a stiff post and rail, which was lower than the fence but quite five feet high. With my heart in my mouth I rode Warrior at this. He made a magnificent bound, cleared it and landed skilfully on all four feet to lessen the jar, for there was a big drop on the other side. As he landed, I was thrown back and accidentally gave him a fearful jab in the mouth with the curb. I hated to have done it, for I knew how much my clumsiness must have hurt his tender mouth. But Warrior did not stop to argue the point with me; he was wild with anger and ran away with me for the first time in his life.

Nothing I could do would stop him. Some people in a gateway were scattered in all directions; fortunately none of them were hurt, but Warrior had no intention of stopping to find that out. He was soon fields away in his determination to punish me for my brutality.

At last he stopped far from the hunt. I jumped off and tried to make much of him, for he was still trembling with rage. I could almost hear him saying: "What a cruel thing to do after the desperate effort I made to land you safely over that great big place!"

I did the best I could, put the reins over his head, and sat down on the ground and let him look at me. At first he tried to break away, but after a bit he calmed down and nibbled a little grass. Then his eye lost its wild look, and again became that beautiful, benevolent orb—the glory of a horse. When he bent down his head to me, and I pulled his ears and put my cheek against his nose, and he licked my hand, I knew we had made it up. It was a long ride home, but we were very happy together again.

Not very long after the War "F. E.," Lord Birkenhead, rented Brooke Hill from me, and brought down his family and three horses to ride and hunt. It was interesting to see the recognition between Birkenhead and Warrior. It will be remembered that they had been together in France in 1914. Those who are interested in horses will know that they have extraordinarily long memories, and Warrior's recognition of "F. E." was a striking instance of it. Aloof as he has always been with grown-up people, he knew his friend of the War at once, and would always walk up to him and stand still to be patted and caressed. I delighted in watching them looking at each other—"F. E." with his grave sombre eyes, and Warrior gazing back at him in quiet friendship.

In the same year we moved to Mottistone, the old manor-house a mile east of Brooke where I write this book, and where Warrior now lives. It took a year to effect the transfer, and, during that time, my tenant, Mr. Jackman, of Mottistone Farm, took charge of Warrior, and his constant companion, Akbar, from whom he had not been separated since 1918.

About a year after we had moved to Mottistone Warrior fell terribly lame in the off-fore, the same leg that had been twisted in the falling house, on

151

the road near Amiens four days later, in 1918, and
again in the sheep netting after the War. I remember
the melancholy conference that we had with "Young
Jim," Aubrey Wykeham, my brother-in-law and
nearest neighbour, and the veterinary surgeon,
Cowper Blake. Warrior was walking about the field
opposite Mottistone Manor, obviously in great pain.
It seemed that the only right thing to do was to end
his troubles.

But Cowper Blake said: "No, I believe the old horse
can be cured."

"Young Jim" added: "If you think so, let us
both have a try." So once again Warrior had a
most narrow escape, this time from the hands of his
friends.

And so it comes about that I can write the story of
a horse still fit and well and gay.

Last year the Colonel of the 2nd Battalion of the
Hampshire Regiment, quartered at Parkhurst, asked
me to take the Salute as His Majesty's representative
at the King's Birthday Parade.

Warrior had been turned out for some months, but
I said that I thought I could have him ready in time.
There were only ten days to tidy him up, but in early
June horses' coats are as glossy as satin if they have not
been clipped. By dint of much grooming Warrior
looked fine when the great day came.

I am sure that those present, including the soldiers
on parade, thought that I steered Warrior with great
skill through all the manoeuvres of taking the Salute
on that day. They were quite wrong. Let me describe

accurately what happened, for it is further proof of
the marvellous memories that horses have.

The Colonel met me at the entrance to the barracks,
and we rode together to the corner of the big sports
field where the battalion was on parade, with a flag
staff in front, and a crowd of spectators beyond.
Now be it observed that Warrior had not attended
more than three military functions since the Victory
Parade in 1919; the episode I describe took place just
seven years after his last previous appearance at a
ceremony of this kind. Of course in his earlier days
Warrior had taken part in many such parades with
me, but I had not thought it possible that he would
remember all about it after the lapse of so many years.
But he did remember, clearly and accurately.

As the Colonel and I on our horses walked towards
the field, Warrior began to lift his forelegs in a kind of
goose step, and arch his neck, clearly conscious of his
fine appearance and what was expected of him. When
he saw the battalion drawn up in line about three
hundred yards away, without any direction from myself, he set to work to canter with a beautiful sweeping
stride right up to the spectators, wheel to his left, canter
a further hundred yards and then, at the same pace,
sweep sharply again to his left in front of the flag staff.
There he drew up and stood like a rock while the due
ceremonial was observed.

It really was a remarkable experience to feel this
old horse, with his strong muscles all taut, rejoicing at
going through the ceremonial which he remembered
so well fourteen, fifteen and sixteen years before, while

I left him to carry through the manœuvre untouched by rein or spur.

During the march past he never moved, eyeing each company as it went by, with head erect and glistening eye. Then came the moment which has caused the downfall of many an inspecting officer. The troops advance in review order. This very often begins to alarm the horse. Then the commanding officer in a loud voice announces that the troops will remove head-dresses, and give three cheers for His Majesty. I have seen many Generals and Staff Officers dislodged by this unexpected shout. But Warrior was much too old a hand for such behaviour that day. I did not say a word to him, for I could see that he knew exactly what was coming. When the great shout went up he just stiffened himself, and stood more smartly at attention.

This, said the Colonel, was the end of the performance, but would I finish by riding along the ranks? It was quite unnecessary for me to decide to do so, for Warrior had already started. When he considered this manœuvre had been properly performed, Warrior knew that the ceremony was indeed over, and cantered straight off the field. His departure was abrupt. I could not have made it otherwise. But, as the Colonel told me, it was most graceful.

This very day on which I write these words, I met two smart soldiers of the Hampshire Regiment as I was riding Warrior through our village. Of course they recognised him, and congratulated me upon his looking so fit and well. They said they remembered

MUNNINGS MADE THIS FIRST STUDY
OF WARRIOR AT TWENTY-SIX YEARS
OF AGE THIS SUMMER. AFTER-
WARDS HE FELT THAT HE HAD
MADE HIS NECK A LITTLE TOO
LONG, SO HE MADE A SECOND.

155

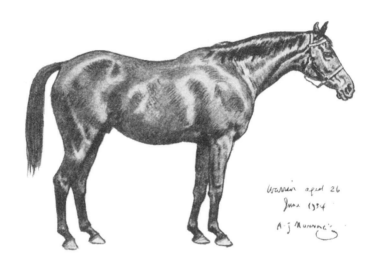

Warrior aged 26
June 1934
A·J·Munnings

HERE IS MUNNINGS'S SECOND STUDY
OF WARRIOR WHICH HE REGARDS
AS A BETTER PORTRAIT. IT IS
WARRIOR TO THE LIFE.

him well from the year before. I asked them if they thought I steered him skilfully to the saluting base; they said "Yes." I said it was not I, it was Warrior that had done the steering. And so, indeed, it was, as the commanding officer, Colonel Perkins, now on the Staff of the Southern Command, will testify.

I had thought at the time that this might well be Warrior's last appearance in public life. But it was not to be so.

When this story of Warrior was well-nigh complete, I received a request to send him to the International Horse Show at Olympia as one of the Veteran War Horses.

It seemed a shame to take him away from the Isle of Wight in the glorious summer weather which he loves so well, but I thought that some people might like to see him, and, anyway, that the old horse would enjoy the adventure.

So, on a morning in June, he was duly embarked on the tow boat at Yarmouth, on his way to Olympia, accompanied by his groom, Bertie White, who succeeded Thomson and has looked after him ever since the War.

I had to make a speech in the Isle of Wight, at Newport, that same afternoon, but I managed to get an aeroplane to take me up to London just in time to meet Warrior on his arrival. It was as well that I did so, for when I found him in the large hall at Olympia he was excited and bothered. He neighed loudly at each of the horses in turn who were putting their heads out of the loose boxes surrounding the hall. I led him myself into the box prepared for him with a legend of his war service nailed on the top.

Next door to him was perhaps the best-known horse in London—Colonel Laurie's grey, which he rides daily through the streets and on all ceremonial occasions.

Warrior did not like the look of him at all, pawed the ground, squealed, snorted and tried to bite him. However, we got him into the box, and gave him a feed. He had been trembling all over when I first met him, but he quietened down after a while.

I was told that there was to be a dress rehearsal that evening, and that the veteran war horses were to be led round by grooms at 10 o'clock. So I went off to dinner and came back at the time named.

There I found Warrior walking round a dimly lit tan riding school, in a state of great perturbation. Beyond a big doorway was the brightly lit arena, with a band playing and sounds of applause. It seemed that Warrior had made up his mind to go no further. Clearly, the only thing to be done was to lead him myself, for he really will go anywhere with me, and I doubted whether anyone else would get him into the ring at all.

While I stood patting his neck in the big doorway he kept on trying to turn away, and was still obviously very much disturbed. Then came a most amusing episode which I shall never forget.

From the ring came the sound of repeated cracks, for all the world like the crackle of rifle-fire. It was the famous stock-whip performance, but its likeness to

MUNNINGS MADE THIS SKETCH OF
WARRIOR ON THE WAY UP TO THE
DOWNS WHILE I WAS TAKING HIM
FOR A RIDE THIS SUMMER.

159

rifle shots was enough for Warrior. Instantly he cocked his ears forward, and it was all I could do to prevent him from getting into the arena, which, a moment before, nothing would have induced him to enter. He said as plainly as if he were talking in our own speech: "I believe there's another war on. Let's go and see what's doing."

In the end I led him round, his eye bright and clear, his neck arched, dancing on his toes like a three-year-old. Nobody knew that I was leading him until the very end, but, at the first sight of him, everyone started to cheer this gay bay thoroughbred, who, at twenty-six years of age, was as capable as ever to rejoice in a new adventure.

I could not see him again for a whole week, but I heard news of him from my friends, for he took part in the parade every day. Just before I had to go abroad I went to see him. As I came into the hall surrounded by loose-boxes, he had got his head out conversing with Colonel Laurie's grey horse, of whom he had now evidently approved, and with whom he had made great friends.

He heard my step and looked up. The door was half open, for the men had been making up his bedding, and he bounded out and trotted towards me, nuzzling up to me with embarrassing affection, rubbing his head against mine, and then putting his head against my cheek. It was indeed a joyful recognition.

At home at Mottistone, I ride him as often as I can. One morning this summer I set off through the village and along the military road to Chilton Chine. There

PEACE

we turned down the long steep steps to the beach. He protested, as well he might, for they are much steeper than the ordinary steps of the Underground railway; but down them he went.

The wind was from the west, as he has always loved it. It was low tide, and there was a great stretch of sand between the red cliffs and the blue sea. As I remounted Warrior he shook himself, and walked straight into the sea, standing there for five minutes or more. Then we turned west towards Mottistone and Brooke. With my daughter Kitty on her pony we galloped on the firm sand for a mile or more, then rode into the sea again till the water was up to the horses' bellies.

How strange and wonderful it was to recapture the glorious joy of a gallop along the sand twenty-four years after the first time that we enjoyed this adventure together!

And so back along the sands, up the lifeboat road at Brooke, and through the village, where many old friends greeted Warrior, to the village school, where the children crowded round him, and rubbed his nose, twenty of them. I told Warrior to look at them one by one, as I knew he would; the children laughed as he eyed them each in turn. And then home to Mottistone, where he has only a small loose box, but is, I know, very happy, as all of us humans are too. He spends most of his time in the same great grass field, within sound of the sea, in which he spent his earliest years.

There we found Munnings, who has made the drawings which illustrate this book. The likeness to

Bartholomew June 11th 1934...

Jackmans field .

HERE IS JACKMAN'S FIELD, THE
PEACEFUL PADDOCK ABOVE THE
SEA WHERE WARRIOR NOW SPENDS
MOST OF HIS SUMMERS AND WHERE
MUNNINGS DREW HIM BENEATH THE
ELMS THIS JUNE, SIXTEEN YEARS
AFTER HIS FIRST PORTRAIT UNDER
VERY DIFFERENT CONDITIONS IN
FRANCE.

163

Warrior is extraordinarily vivid, as all who know him
will testify.

Munnings wrote this to me after his visit:

"My first portrait of Warrior was done in mud and
frost and east wind, under much discomfort and in a
hurry, in 1918. My second portrait was made under
very different conditions sixteen years later.

"The old horse, still a picture, is living with a chestnut friend, in wide peaceful paddocks with tall elms
in full leaf, the buttercups a yellow blaze, the gorse
on the downs, and the sea in the distance.

"Instead of a few hours in the perishing cold, this
time we had days of leisure in the warm June sun, with
blackbirds singing, and turtle doves cooing up in the
elms.

"I think Warrior a grand type of horse. The sixteen
years have passed lightly over him. His legs are still
clean. A wonderfully girthed horse, and a good
pattern to study."

Here you see him, as Munnings has drawn him, in
his paddock above the sea, able to gaze across the
Channel towards France, where he helped to make
history sixteen years ago.

It is, I know, remarkable that a man should be able
to write about a horse who has been his constant and
intimate friend, in peace and in war, for more than a
quarter of a century.

But Warrior is in himself remarkable. He could not
have earned the tributes of admiration and affection,
some of which I have quoted, from men like John

French, Freddie Guest, Geoffrey Brooke, Major Hall, Archie Macdonnell and hundreds, even thousands, of Canadian soldiers unless he had been of a strange and arresting quality.

All these years of our comradeship have set me wondering what was the secret of Warrior's quality and character; especially have I so wondered since I began to write this book.

I think I know the reason. It is not his ancestry, interesting though that is; it is not some quite peculiar quality differentiating him from other horses of his time; these no doubt are factors, but not the chief factors.

I am persuaded that the real reason why he has thus impressed his personality and character upon all those who have been brought into contact with him, in peace and in war, is the fact that he has never been ill-treated, never badly used, never beaten when he was doing his best.

The soul of a horse is a great and loyal soul, quite unspoiled by the chances and changes of human kind. Above all, it is a courageous soul, and an affectionate soul. But let there be one cruel blow from a grown-up man, and you have ruined the horse's fine soul and spirit for ever.

It is my dream that those who read this book may vow never to beat a willing horse.

Warrior has never been so beaten, partly by good fortune, partly because it takes a brave man to beat him. And so it comes about that I can write of him as possessing an absolutely faithful and fearless soul.

As I have recounted, he is the darling of all the children amongst whom he lives. They all come up to him and stroke his head as he turns his benevolent eye on them. For he knows every one of those around him quite intimately, as they know him. Though I have known him for so long, I can still learn from observing my old horse, now so experienced and so wise in his relation to men and things, after his long and varied life.

He is more good-humoured with strangers than he used to be, but still aloof. Each day he gets more and more devoted to his intimate friends. More touching than anything else about him is his affection for my wife. Always when he sees her he will walk up to her, lay his soft nose against her cheek, and close his eyes— the supreme tribute of friendship from a horse to a human being.

Twenty-six years of intimate friendship with such a horse is a privilege granted to very few, but it has been mine.

EPILOGUE

Warrior continued on his much loved way until the fates caught up with him in the wartime spring of 1941. By then conditions even in the Isle of Wight were very different from the summer days when Alfred Munnings worked his magic. The old horse was now 33 – though his obituaries reproduced on page 172 give his age as 32, since he was a few weeks short of his actual birthday when he died – and needed a daily supply of corn, which created some mutterings as human rationing bit. As Lord Lieutenant of Hampshire, Jack Seely bowed to the inevitable but stipulated that the end should come when he was away as he could not bear to be there for the closing.

There is no grave. A few years ago I spoke with an old man who as a farmer's boy had seen the vet arrive and the knacker's van come and go. "You must remember it was wartime," he said, "everything was needed. Even Warrior."

But why make a record of his death when where he lived is so much with us? The downs and farms and beaches of the western side of the Isle of Wight are still not that far removed from Warrior's time. Walk or ride on Compton Down, look across at the Solent on one side and the Channel on the other, and you are drinking in the same views, treading the same turf as Jack and Warrior did all those years ago. Take the road down to Brooke Church and on the right is Sidling Paul, the sloping field in which Warrior passed his boyhood and which Munnings so beautifully illustrated in this book. What's more that very same barn has now been renovated by my cousin Patrick Seely and the success of this book has funded a magnificent Philip Blacker bronze of Warrior and his rider which now stands in the Isle of Wight as a tribute to the horse which brought his homeland so much glory. In July 2014 the statue was

167

STATUE OF WARRIOR BY PHILIP BLACKER ON DISPLAY AT CARISBROOKE CASTLE
ON THE ISLE OF WIGHT.

unveiled within the historic keep of Carisbrooke Castle, not five miles from where Warrior lived all his life bar one remarkable four year interlude between 1914 and 1918. In September 2014 his gallantry was officially commemorated with the award of the PDSA's Dickin Medal, "the animals' VC".

My grandfather lived on until 1947, but don't doubt that Warrior's passing affected him greatly. One cold morning when I was doing the research for *Galloper Jack* I found a document amongst his papers at Nuffield College, Oxford. It was a diary entry from Good Friday 1941. "I do not believe," he wrote about Warrior's death, "to quote Byron about his dog Boatswain, 'that he can be denied in heaven the soul that he held on earth.'"

May this book help that soul to live on.

BROUGH SCOTT
July 2014

THE FIRST WORLD WAR

KEY DATES AND TIMELINE

28 June 1914 –The assassination of Archduke Franz Ferdinand
The assassination of the heir to the Austro-Hungarian throne led
to several complex alliances, formed over previous decades, being
invoked. Within weeks the major European powers were at war both
in Europe and worldwide via their colonies.

28 July 1914 – The beginning of the First World War
The Austro-Hungarian alliance declared war on Serbia on 28 July
1914. In August, Germany invaded Belgium and Luxembourg and
opened up the notorious Western Front. Britain declared war with
Germany on 4 August 1914. The USA stayed neutral until 6 April
1917.

1915–1918 – Stalemate on the Western Front
The Western Front, which stretched 440 miles from the North Sea
in Belgium across France to the Swiss border, was the most famous
of all fronts in the First World War.

Amongst the major offensives on the Western Front were:
Battle of the Frontiers   August 1914
First Battle of the Marne   September 1914
First Battle of Ypres   October – November 1914
Second Battle of Ypres   April – May 1915
Battle of Verdun   February – December 1916
Battle of the Somme   July – November 1916
Battle of Arras   April – May 1917
Third Battle of Ypres   July – November 1917

11 November 1918 – The end of the First World War
Four major empires – the German, Russian, Austro-Hungarian and
Ottoman – were defeated and ceased to exist.

170

HORSES IN THE FIRST WORLD WAR

- When the war began in 1914, the British Army possessed a mere 25,000 horses
- The War Office was immediately tasked with finding another half a million to go into battle
- As well as serving in the cavalry, they were needed to transport weapons and supplies and to carry the dying and wounded to hospital
- During the war, the main source of horses came from the United States, and between 1914 and 1917 around 1,000 were sent by ship every day – with these ships under constant enemy attack
- In battle, horses were vulnerable to artillery and machine-gun fire as well as to the harsh winter conditions on the front line
- The losses were appallingly high and mirrored the human losses in the terrible battles of the Somme and Passchendaele
- Of the one million horses sent to the Western Front by Britain, over 900,000 did not return home
- It is estimated that over eight million horses, donkeys and mules died in total in the First World War
- With the involvement of the RSPCA and the Royal Army Veterinary Corps, the care of horses during the war improved immeasurably with the creation of special veterinary hospitals by the British Army
- Due to the development of tanks and the evolution of warfare, the First World War would be the last time the horse would be used on a mass scale in modern conflict

171

The Times
5 April 1941

"MY HORSE WARRIOR"

DEATH OF A WELL-KNOWN CHARGER

Warrior, Lord Mottistone's old charger, has died at Mottistone Manor, in the Isle of Wight. His age was 32. The severe weather of the last two winters had affected his health, and Lord Mottistone regretfully decided to have the horse painlessly destroyed.

Lord Mottistone told his story in " My Horse Warrior," which he published in 1934. Bred by his life-long owner from a thoroughbred mare named Cinderella, Warrior became a good-looking, powerful bay standing 15.2. Lord Mottistone took him to France as part of the original Expeditionary Force in 1914. He was soon in the retreat from Mons with the G.H.Q. horses. At the Marne and again during the First Battle of Ypres he was often ridden by the Commander-in-Chief, Sir John French.

When Lieutenant-Colonel Seely, as he then was, was appointed early in 1915 to command the Canadian Cavalry Brigade he returned to England with Warrior to complete the training of his new command. After that interlude the horse served continuously on the Western Front till Christmas Day, 1918. Twice he was buried by the bursting of big shells on soft ground, but he was never seriously wounded. The Canadians, all of whom held Warrior in great affection, called him. " The horse the Germans can't kill." His owner afterwards said, " His escapes were quite wonderful. Again and again he survived when death seemed certain and, indeed, befell all his neighbours. It was not all hazard ; sometimes it was due to his intelligence. I have seen him, even when a shell has burst within a few feet, stand still without a tremor—just turn his head and, unconcerned, look at the smoke of the burst."

After 1918 Warrior became the family hunter in the land of his birth, the Isle of Wight. From time to time his owner gave news of his welfare to the readers of The Times. In his last letter on the subject, dated May 31, 1938, Lord Mottistone announced that that morning they had cantered together over Mottistone Downs, " greatly rejoicing, our united ages being exactly 100 years." Warrior's portrait was painted by Mr. A. J. Munnings several times—the first time in France with the Canadian Cavalry Brigade. His last ceremonial appearance was in the parade of veteran war-horses at the Horse Show at Olympia seven years ago.

Horse the Germans Could Not Kill

Lord Mottistone's famous old war horse Warrior, which he and Sir John French (Lord Ypres) rode during the last war, has died at Mottistone Manor, Isle of Wight, at the age of 32.

Warrior had so many narrow escapes from death in the last war that the Canadian cavalry, whom Lord Mottistone commanded in France, used to call him " the horse the Germans can't kill."

Evening Standard
4 April 1941

INDEX

WARRIOR

174

INDEX

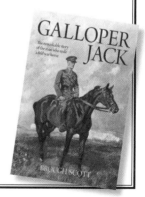

Whittlebury June 11th 1834(?)

Jackmans field.